William Shakespeare

A Midsummer Night's Dream

Edited by

John Russell Brown

*With Theatre
Commentary by
John Hirsch and Leslie Thomson*

APPLAUSE
NEW YORK • LONDON

The Applause Shakespeare Library
A Midsummer Night's Dream
Editor and General Series Editor: John Russell Brown
Commentary by Leslie Thomson and John Hirsch
Copyright © 1996 Applause Books

Library of Congress Cataloging-in-Publication Data

Shakespeare, William, 1564-1616.
    A Midsummer Night's Dream/ William Shakespeare ; edited by John Hirsch and Leslie Thomson
      p.   cm. — (The Applause Shakespeare library)
    Includes bibliographical references.
    ISBN 1-55783-181-5 : $7.95
    I. Hirsch, John 1930-   II. Thomson, Leslie.   III. Title.
IV. Series.
PR2827.A2H53   1994
822.3'3—dc20   94-30104
                                                       CIP

British Library Cataloging-in-Publication Data

A catalog record for this book is available from the British Library.

Applause Books
211 West 71st Street
New York, NY 10023
Phone (212) 496-7511
Fax: (212) 721-2856

406 Vale Road
Tonbridge Kent TN9 1XR
Phone 073 235-7755
Fax 073 207-7219

Cover photo from the Stratford Festival Production of *A Midsummer Night's Dream*, Stratford, Ontario, 1984, Directed by John Hirsch; Photograph by David Cooper.
From left: Danny Kohn (Cobweb), Patricia Connolly (Titania), Nicholas Pennell (Oberon), Diego Matamoros (Puck)

Table of Contents

The Applause Shakespeare Library

Titles now Available:

King Lear
Macbeth
A Midsummer Night's Dream
The Tempest

Other Titles in Preparation

Antony and Cleopatra
Hamlet
Henry V
Julius Caesar
Measure for Measure
The Merchant of Venice
Othello
Romeo and Juliet
Twelfth Night

General Preface to the Applause Shakespeare Library

This edition is designed to help readers see and hear the plays in action. It gives an impression of how actors can bring life to the text and shows how certain speeches, movements, or silences take on huge importance once the words have left the page and become part of a performance. It is a theatrical edition, like no other available at this time.

Everyone knows that Shakespeare wrote for performance and not for solitary readers or students in classrooms. Yet the great problem of how to publish the plays so that readers can understand their theatrical life is only beginning to be tackled. Various solutions have been tried. The easiest—and it is an uneasy compromise—is to commission some director or leading actor to write a preface about the play in performance and print that at the beginning of the volume, followed by a critical and historical introduction, the text and notes about verbal difficulties, a textual introduction, and a collation of variant readings as in any other edition. Another easy answer is to supply extensive stage directions to sort out how characters enter or exit and describe any gestures or actions that the text explicitly requires. Both methods give the reader little or no help in realizing the play in performance, moment by moment, as the text is read.

A more thorough-going method is to include some notes about staging and acting among the annotations of meaning, topical references, classical allusions, textual problems, and so forth. The snag here is that the theatrical details make no consecutive sense and cannot deal with the larger issues of the build-up of conflict or atmosphere, the developing impression of character, or the effect of group and individual movement on stage. Such notes offer, at best, intermittent assistance.

In the more expensive one-volume editions, with larger-than-usual formats, yet another method is used—to include a stage history of the play showing how other ages have staged the play and describing a few recent productions that have been more than usually successful with the critics. The snag here is that unavailable historical knowledge is required to interpret records of earlier performances. Moreover, the journalistic accounts of productions which are quoted in these histories are liable to emphasize what is unusual in a production rather than the opportunities offered to actors in any production of the play, the text's enduring theatrical vitality. In any case, all this material is kept separate from the rest of the book and not easily consulted during a reading of the text.

The Applause Shakespeare goes further than any of these. It does the usual tasks expected of a responsible, modern edition, but adds a very special feature: a continuous commentary on the text by a professional director or a leading actor that considers the stage life of the play as its action unfolds. It shows what is demanded from the actors—line by line where necessary—and points out what decisions about interpretation have to be made and the consequences of one choice over another. It indicates where emotional climaxes are placed—and where conflicting thoughts in the character's mind create subtextual pressures beneath the words. Visual statements are noted: the effect of groups of figures on stage, of an isolated figure, or of a pair of linked figures in a changing relationship; the effect of delayed or unexpected entries, sudden departures, slow or processional exeunts, or a momentarily empty stage. Everything that happens on stage comes within the notice of this commentary. A reader can "feel" what the play would be like in action.

What the commentary does not do is equally important from the reader's point of view. It does not try to provide a single theatrical reading of the text. Rather if offers a range of possibilities, a number of suggestions as to what an actor might do. Performances cannot be confined to a single, unalterable realization: rather, each production is continually discovering new potential in a text, and it is this power of revelation and revaluation that the commentary of the Applause Shakespeare seeks to open up to individual readers. With this text in hand, the play can be produced in the theatre of the mind, creating a performance suitable to the moment and responsive to individual imaginations. As stimulus for such recreations, the commentary sometimes describes the choices that particular actors or directors made in famous productions, showing what effect words or physical performances have achieved. The purpose here is to supplement what a reader might supply from his or her own experience and imagination, and also to suggest ways in which further research might discover more about the text's theatrical life.

The commentary is printed in a wide column on the page facing the text itself, so that reference can be quickly made at any particular point or, alternatively, so that the commentary can be read as its own narrative of the play in action. Also, to the right of the text are explanations of difficult words, puns, multiple meanings, topical allusions, references to other texts, etc. All of these things will be found in other editions, but here it is readily accessible without the eye having to seek out the foot of the page or notes bunched together at the rear of the volume. The text is modernized in spelling. Both stage directions and punctuation are kept to a minimum—enough to make reading easy, but not so elaborate that readers are prevented from giving life to the text in whatever way they choose. As an aid to reading aloud, speech-prefixes are printed in full and extra space used to set speeches apart from each other; when the text is read silently, each new voice can register clearly. At the rear of the book, an extended note explains the authority for the text and a collation gives details of variant readings and emendations.

In many ways the Applause Shakespeare is a pioneering edition, responding to an old challenge in a new way and trying to break down barriers to understanding that have proved very obstinate for a long time. Further volumes are in preparation and editorial procedures are being kept under review. Reports on the usefulness of the edition, and especially of its theatrical commentary, would be most welcome. Please write to John Russell Brown, c/o Applause Books, 1841 Broadway, Suite 1100, New York, NY 10023.

INTRODUCTION

Belief in fairies is rare in our times, even among the smallest children, but Shakespeare's *A Midsummer Night's Dream*, which is presided over by Oberon and Titania, King and Queen of fairies, and which is full of magic and enchantment, is still read and performed throughout the world. The reason is that the fairies in this play are not simply a self-contained, miniature, and pretty tribe of creatures, not unlike human beings but usually invisible to mortal eyes. Shakespeare saw them like that in his mind's eye, and yet as much more besides.

Most of Shakespeare's contemporaries did believe that there were spirits of all sorts alive in the world and existing in its various elements of earth, air, fire, and water. They called them many different names, such as sprites, goblins, daemons, devils, elves, spirits, creatures, and fairies. Water-devils or naiads were sometimes called fairies; according to some authorities, they had a queen and

> cause inundations, many times shipwrecks, and deceive men in diverse ways, as *succubae* or otherwise, appearing most part in women's shapes...

That is Robert Burton's account in *The Anatomy of Melancholy*, first published in 1621 and drawing together the opinions of many former writers. Spirits living in earth included "lares, genii, fauns, satyres, wood-nymphs, foliots, fairies, Robin Goodfellows, trolls." Burton recalled how these have

> been in former times adored with much superstition, with sweeping their houses, and setting a pail of clean water, good victuals and the like...These are they that dance on heaths and greens.

Sometimes they would lead mortals to their hiding-places and show them marvelous sights. Paracelsus, a renowned German scholar of the early sixteenth century, reported that they had been seen walking in little coats, some two foot long. Ludwig Lavater, whose treatise *Of Ghosts and Spirits Walking by Night* was translated into English in 1572, said that these pucks or pooks "draw men out of the way, and lead them all night a by-way, or quite bar them of their way."

But not every Elizabethan believed in fairies. The notes to Edmund Spenser's early poem, *The Shepheard's Calendar* (1579), are forthright in condemning such supersition:

> the opinion of fairies and elves is very old, and yet sticketh very religiously in the minds of some. But to root that rank opinion of

elves out of men's hearts, the truth is that there be no such things,
nor yet the shadows of the things.

Such absolute dissent was not common however, for while doubts were
often expressed about the actual existence of these spirits, it was a most
respectable opinion that men could *imagine* that they saw such creatures.
This idea is crucial for understanding Shakespeare's use of fairies and of
many other magic and supernatural events in the plays. His non-human
beings are "shadows," or outward expressions of thoughts and feelings, the
means to represent almost nameless fears and excitements, and almost intan-
gible sensations.

Shakespeare's characters speak about fairies when their imaginations or
fantasies are seething with possibilities and doubts, and with images which
transcend or ignore the ordinary affairs of life. In *The Comedy of Errors*,
Dromio of Syracuse arrives in Ephesus to find himself ordered about by a
fine lady he has never seen before, so that he hardly knows what is happening and falls to his prayers: "O, for my beads! I cross me for a sinner!" But
this changes nothing and he is precipitated towards superstitious fantasy:

This is fairy land. O spite of spites!
We talk with goblins, owls, and sprites.
If we obey them not, this will ensue:
They'll suck our breath, or pinch us black and blue.   (II.ii.187–90)

He says, and his master agrees with him, that he has been "transformed,"
altered out of all recognition by magic; he believes that he has been changed
into an "ass."

In *Romeo and Juliet*, Shakespeare's hero is unwilling to go to a ball
because he has had a bad dream. His friend, Mercutio, says at once that this
is fairies' work:

O then I see Queen Mab hath been with you.
She is the fairies' midwife, and she comes
In shape no bigger than an agate stone
On the fore-finger of an alderman,
Drawn with a team of little atomies,
Over men's noses as they lie asleep;...   (I.iv.53–58)

Mercutio goes on to ascribe to Queen Mab the power to reflect the inward
thoughts of all sorts of people, functioning differently for each according to
their preoccupations, whether courtier, lawyer, lady, parson, soldier, or whatever. When he starts to speak of young girls who dream of love-making,
Romeo interrupts the flight of fantasy with

> Peace, peace, Mercutio, peace!
> Thou talk'st of nothing.

"True," comes the answer:

> I talk of dreams,
> Which are the children of an idle brain,
> Begot of nothing but vain fantasy. (I.iv.94–97)

The existence of fairies could be discussed seriously in Shakespeare's day, but, like dreams, their credibility depended on the eye and mind of the beholder. At the close of *A Midsummer Night's Dream*, Puck, who belongs to the play's fairy kingdom and yet interferes often in mortal affairs, steps forward to say:

> If we shadows have offended,
> Think but this, and all is mended:
> That you have but slumb'red here
> While these visions did appear.
> And this weak and idle theme,
> No more yielding but a dream,
> Gentles, do not reprehend. (V.i.404–10)

Puck speaks of "shadows"—reflections of humankind, images, insubstantial beings, dark shapes attending substantial bodies—the same word that is found in the notes of *The Shepheard's Calendar*. When the lovers in the *Dream* wake in the wood where they have been misled and enchanted by Puck, Demetrius thinks everything has been a dream, and still is a dream:

> Are you sure
> That we are awake? It seems to me
> That yet we sleep, we dream. (IV.i.188–90)

This is exactly what Puck asks the audience to think, and what Oberon had foretold: the mortals would

> think no more of this night's accidents
> But as the fierce vexation of a dream. (IV.i.64–65)

The King of fairies seems unaware that some of his victims would find their dream to be sweet or wonderful, and "past the wit of man to say what dream it was" (IV.i.201–02).

Shakespeare's association of dreams and fairies was fully in accord with renaissance psychology. The inward senses were thought to be of three kinds: common sense, fantasy, and memory. "Fantasy" is that capacity of mind which can cause a person to think he or she sees strange, monstrous, and absurd things when these do not actually exist and have no objective reality. Although most active when dreaming, fantasy can dominate consciousness whenever the hold of "common sense" (or "reason") is relaxed and so fails to exercise its usual control. The "seething brains" of lovers, as they are called in this play, were said to be among the most apt to imagine that they see fantastic and unreal sights, and to believe that they have been transported to strange worlds or transformed into new shapes. When learned men debated whether love was seated in the heart, liver, or fantasy, they usually pronounced in favor of the fantasy, or, as some would say, the imagination.

A Midsummer Night's Dream is about fairies and enchantment, but, more than this, it is a comedy about the imagination. Much of its action takes place at night when fantasy is most active. Its human characters are seized by love, anger, or ambition; some are the prey of fairies and act in the strangest and most headlong ways, and others of their own free will enact a fantastic play about heroic love. When the lovers have escaped from the enchanted wood and are prepared for marriage, Duke Theseus, who is himself a bridegroom, recognizes the truth of the strange events he has been told, not because he believes in fairies but because it is true to his experience of what lovers, lunatics, and poets can imagine:

> Lovers and madmen have such seething brains,
> Such shaping fantasies, that apprehend
> More than cool reason ever comprehends.
> The lunatic, the lover and the poet
> Are of imagination all compact.
> One sees more devils than vast hell can hold:
> That is the madman. The lover, all as frantic,
> Sees Helen's beauty in a brow of Egypt.
> The poet's eye, in a fine frenzy rolling,
> Doth glance from heaven to earth, from earth to heaven;
> And as imagination bodies forth
> The forms of things unknown, the poet's pen
> Turns them to shapes and gives to airy nothing
> A local habitation and a name.
> Such tricks hath strong imagination
> That, if it would but apprehend some joy,
> It comprehends some bringer of that joy;
> Or in the night, imagining some fear,
> How easy is a bush supposed a bear!   (V.i.4–22)

The lovers and the fairies of the *Dream* use similar verbal images, and act with similar speed, lightness, changeability, and unreflecting cruelty, and the play's poet-dramatist seems to have been equally at home with both groups of characters.

The supernatural characters of the play are not of any strict lineage. Oberon and Titania inhabit the world of classical myth and are thus associated with the power of natural phenomena. Through their "distemperature" we see

> The seasons alter: hoary-headed frosts
> Fall in the fresh lap of the crimson rose,
> And on old Hiems' thin and icy crown
> An odorous chaplet of sweet summer buds
> Is, as in mockery, set.   (II.i.107–11)

But they are also denizens of the English countryside and, with their troops of followers, they quarrel, dance, and process through green woods and flowery fields. Their servants hang dewdrops in cowslips' ears and steal light from glowworms and the painted wings of butterflies. These more domestic functions belong to a folk tradition, derided by King James in his treatise on *Daemonology* (1597):

> How there was a King and Queen of fairy, of such a jolly court
> and train as they had; how they had a tend [or tythe] and duty, as
> it were, of all goods; how they naturally rode and went, ate and
> drank, and did all other actions like natural men and women.

Yet Oberon and Titania outstep this tradition too, being more than self-concerned: they also attend the nuptials of mortals and wish blessings on them, as spirits of fecundity have done according to folklore in many countries across the world. More than this, they inhabit the elegant and golden world of pastoral poetry:

> And in the shape of Corin sat all day,
> Playing on pipes of corn and versing love
> To amorous Philida.   (II.i.66–68)

In this guise they represent a dream of simplicity and fulfillment.

Puck, or Robin Goodfellow as he is also called, stands out from the other fairies in the *Dream* by being in a more clearly rustic and domestic folk tradition, as he explains on his first entrance (see II.i.34–57). He enjoys mere pranks, and the waste of merry hours. But he also has other shapes, attending Oberon dutifully and chasing the "rude mechanicals" out of the wood in the appearance of frightening monsters:

> Sometime a horse I'll be, sometime a hound,
> A hog, a headless bear, sometime a fire;

> And neigh, and bark, and grunt, and roar, and burn,
>> Like horse, hound, hog, bear, fire, at every turn. (III.i.94–97)

What is common to all Shakespeare's supernatural characters is not a consistent other-world which they inhabit, but rather their ability to express the teeming richness and captivating power of human imagination. Bottom, the weaver, who is snatched precipitously into the loving care of Titania, experiences the most tender, exquisite, and harmonious fairy love:

> I'll give thee fairies to attend on thee,
> And they shall fetch thee jewels from the deep,
> And sing while thou on pressed flowers dost sleep;
> And I will purge thy mortal grossness so,
> That thou shalt like an airy spirit go. (III.i.137–41)

Later the Queen of fairies takes Bottom in her arms:

> So doth the woodbine the sweet honeysuckle
> Gently entwist; the female ivy so
> Enrings the barky fingers of the elm.

And she concludes like a mortal lover, herself overwhelmed with the new experience, almost at a loss for words:

> O how I love thee! How I dote on thee! (IV.i.38–41)

Bottom attempts to respond in a courtly manner, but soon he complains of itches and hunger, and then falls asleep. (He is not unlike the drunken tinker, Christopher Sly, in *The Taming of the Shrew*, who, being given an illusion of riches and married life, and a play to make him laugh, falls unceremoniously into silence and then perhaps to oblivious sleep.) But when Bottom wakes from his "dream," something remains in his fuddled brain, a wonder that shatters all normal understanding. To express this consciousness, Shakespeare gives to his clumsy but adventurous weaver the words that St. Paul had used in speaking of the love of God. In the Bishops' Bible, Shakespeare's contemporaries would read that

> The eye hath not seen, and the ear hath not heard, neither have
> entered into the heart of man, the things which God hath pre-
> pared for them that love him. (*I Corinthians*, II.9)

What Bottom says is:

> The eye of man hath not heard, the ear of man hath not seen,
> man's hand is not able to taste, his tongue to conceive,
> nor his heart to report, what my dream was. (IV.i.206–09)

He cannot describe his fairy experience, except insofar as he had been an ass; but his fantasy retains a glimmering sense of wonder, glory, and humility, because in some sense the dream was his own.

When the play's action leaves the wood and returns to Athens, Shakespeare still has not finished with his exploration of imaginative reality. As the uncultured "mechanicals" struggle to perform their uncouth and lofty play, growing in self-confidence and absurdity, Theseus and his queen come to realise the extent to which imaginative involvement can find a response and justification only by an answering imaginative acceptance:

> HIPPOLYTA: This is the silliest stuff that ever I heard.
> THESEUS: The best in this kind are but shadows; and the worst are no
>   worse, if imagination amend them.
> HIPPOLYTA: It must be your imagination then, and not theirs.
> THESEUS: If we imagine no worse of them than they of themselves,
>   they may pass for excellent men. Here come two noble beasts in,
>   a man and a lion.   (V.i.206–12)

The opposite—the exposure and pain which an unequal response can bring—is shown as Starveling, enacting the role of Moonshine, is mocked and humiliated by the young lovers. This audience can catch no resemblance between their fantasies and that which the stumbling actor attempts to display.

When Puck holds the stage to speak an epilogue, after the players have danced off stage and the lovers have gone to bed, he offers the audience an awareness of their own mortality, beyond any previous fantasy in the comedy:

> Now the hungry lion roars,
>   And the wolf behowls the moon;
> Whilst the heavy plowman snores,
>   All with weary task fordone.
> Now the wasted brands do glow,
>   Whilst the screech owl, screeching loud,
> Puts the wretch that lies in woe
>   In remembrance of a shroud...   (V.i.352–59)

After this dark moment, the fairies reenter in procession, carrying lights and singing, and the various imaginative transformations of *A Midsummer Night's Dream* end in delight.

*   *   *

Duke Theseus and his bride Hippolyta are almost untouched by the fairy enchantment of the play, but he does sense its presence towards the close of the play:

> The iron tongue of midnight hath told twelve:
> Lovers, to bed; 'tis almost fairy time. (V.i.344–45)

From the start he is in charge of the main action of the comedy, with the power to support Egeus in his demand that as father he should be able to "dispose" of his daughter Hermia to the young man of his choice, Demetrius, and not to Lysander whom she loves. Yet, in offering Hermia an alternative to death, which is the punishment her father calls for if she refuses Demetrius, Theseus seems more aware than Egeus of another's suffering and of the mysteries of the natural order of things:

> if you yield not to your father's choice
> You can endure the livery of a nun,
> For aye to be in shady cloister mewed,
> To live a barren sister all your life,
> Chanting faint hymns to the cold fruitless moon. (I.i.69–73)

In his own life Theseus has experienced the "vexations" of love and enchantment. His bride is the Amazon and warrior Queen, Hippolyta, whom he had first conquered in battle. He has had many loves and Oberon says that he has been enchanted by Titania:

> Didst not thou lead him through the glimmering night
> From Perigenia, whom he ravished?
> And make him with fair Aegles break his faith,
> With Ariadne, and Antiopa? (II.i.77–80)

When Theseus arrives with his bride in the wood on the first of May and finds four young lovers sleeping, he is quick to sense the "gentle concord" that has been forged and the latent comedy of the situation. He orders that all of them should be married in the temple along with himself and sets aside his earlier judgement against Hermia.

With a poet's imagination, Shakespeare has provided a strange accompaniment for Theseus and Hippolyta as they enter the wood after the fairies have disappeared and the sun has risen on their wedding day. First there is the sound of hunting horns (IV.i.98,S.D.) and then appreciative talk of the "gallant chiding" (l. 111) of Spartan hounds, "crook-kneed and dew-lapped like Thessalian bulls"(l. 118). Theseus does not wake the sleepers himself but gives orders for offstage activity: there is a stage direction, which is probably Shakespeare's own, calling for "*Shout within*" and then for "*Wind horns*" as the lovers are awakened and all "*start up*"(l. 134). So the lovers are woken from sleep by the sounds of hounds newly roused and in full cry—an aural representation, provided by Theseus, of a terror that would strike fear before provoking laughter. However pleasurable to their owners' ears—according to Hippolyta, "I never heard/So musical a discord, such sweet thunder"—this was a cry to set a bear at bay rather than to accompany the "wood-birds" as they begin to couple (11. 135–36). A tolerant Theseus can match the "fierce vexation" of a dream with the sound of his Spartan hounds, as he witnesses the change of fortune in young lovers' pursuit of happiness. His device may serve to awaken the play's audience in the theatre just as surprisingly, making them wonder, for the moment at least, what strange beasts are about to unsettle the pleasures of the play's ending.

The young lovers do not have Theseus' "common sense" and long "memory" to keep their "fantasies" in check. They love and hate, fly and pursue, with absolute belief in the validity of their responses: Hermia is "bold" in confronting Theseus to a degree which she does not understand (I.i.59); Helena,

> sweet lady, dotes
> Devoutly dotes, dotes in idolatry,
> Upon this spotted and inconstant man   (I.i.108–10)

—that is, upon Demetrius, who has changed his allegiance to Hermia. They know that "quick bright things come to confusion," and that "true lovers have been ever crossed"; but they scarcely hesitate in their various commitments, taking all difficulties

> As due to love as thoughts and dreams and sighs,
> Wishes, and tears, poor Fancy's followers. (I.i.154–55)

In the wood their antics are wild before they come in contact with any of the fairies. Magic enchantment, caused by Oberon's spell, seems only to catapult them in new directions. Swords are drawn in anger, tears shed, insults exchanged, oaths sworn, arms clasped tightly around unwilling victims, fingers prepared to gouge out eyes; mocking, bitter, loving, earnest, self-effacing, amazed, and cruel words follow each other with bewildering speed. By good fortune, as well as self-assertion, they are separated, and Puck can sort them out and sedate them, so that all will be at peace when they awake to the yelping hounds.

The fourth group of characters, the "rude mechanicals" who meet in the wood to rehearse "most obscenely and courageously" (I.ii.88–89), are not under Theseus's control until their play, *The most lamentable comedy and most cruel death of Pyramus and Thisbe*, is presented as part of the celebrations of his nuptials at court. Without any encouragement or restraint, their antics are just as funny, but by no means as violent, as those of the lovers. Rather they are marked by considerable discretion, and by concern that they might "fright the ladies out of their wits" (I.ii.64–65) —it is for that they fear they might be hanged, not for loving the wrong person. Nevertheless, dramatic ambition does awaken their imaginations or fantasies, and their absurdities become incessant.

As they prepare themselves for their various heroic roles, Nick Bottom the weaver is most at home and fearless; and it is on him that Puck plays his trick, placing an ass's head on his shoulders. In turn this causes Titania, on whom Oberon has cast his love-spell, to find him alone and fall in love with him. In their scenes together the tenderness, humility, courtesy, and boundless generosity of love are made most fully apparent. Bottom never loses his absurdity, but from the moment he is alone in the wood and decides to sing so "that they shall hear I am not afraid"(III.i.107), he lives up to whatever unfolds so amazingly before him and to whomever touches his uncomprehending body. He seems to travel further and more successfully in his "dream" than any other person in the play. His performance in *Pyramus and Thisbe* when its time comes has also an outsize vigor and unabated imaginative involvement, even though he steps out of his role to explain what the audience should have understood for themselves, and even though he contrives to die several times and to rise from the dead.

The scenes involving these

> Hard-handed men that work in Athens here,
> Which never labored in their minds till now   (V.i.72–73)

are the most original in the entire play. Shakespeare has filled their dialogue and activity with many shrewdly observed details of day-to-day life and many indications of the awakening of imaginative involvement, wonder, and generosity of spirit. They are led by Peter Quince who can neither stand up to Bottom's demands nor speak the Prologue to the play with any sensible discretion, but they achieve their ambitions, raise and quell laughter, and triumph at the end of the comedy in a dance which takes the place of a more conventional dance of reconciled lovers or of more general festivities. But then, a few moments later, when the Duke and "all his train" have left in silence, it is the fairies who take over for yet another dance and song, which are beyond the talents of any mortals to join.

*   *   *

A Midsummer Night's Dream is most cunningly contrived. It has no one source to provide its narrative drive, as do all Shakespeare's other comedies, except *The Tempest*. It seems to have been designed to explore a great web of sensations and thoughts, all concerned with imagination and its conflicts with common sense, so that incidents flow after each other with almost the same ease as image follows image in a dream, or in some of the jewelled and fluent verse which is another mark of this comedy. Yet it is all so finely balanced that a very deliberate artifice seems to lie behind its most wayward incidents.

In Act V there is one clear sign of Shakespeare's concern for careful balance. Theseus speaking of imagination in an early draft had referred only to the lover and the madman. The "poet" and his "fine frenzy" were added later. (In the technical language of the time, "frenzy" was a more severe form of madness than the merely "frantic.") Mislineation in the early printed editions is here accounted for by supposing some passages were added in the margin as second thoughts, so that Theseus was originally to say, not the speech as quoted on page viii of this introduction, but as follows:

> Lovers and madmen have such seething brains,
> Such shaping fantasies that apprehend
> More than cool reason ever comprehends.
> One sees more devils than vast hell can hold;
> That is the madman. The lover, all as frantic,
> Sees Helen's beauty in a brow of Egypt.
> Such tricks hath strong imagination,
> That if it would but apprehend some joy,
> It comprehends some bringer of that joy.

The delicate and complicated balance of this play means that it is full of strange reflections, from one world to another, from the established certainties of Theseus's court to the headlong freedom of young lovers as they escape to the woods, to the amateur theatricals of the workmen from Athens, to the worlds of fable and poetic imitation, to the nightmares of superstition and horror, to the strange images of sexual arousal, and to the fascinating and improbable miniature world of the fairies, to delicate beauties of the English countryside, to violence in battle and the chase, and to the power of poetry.

Shakespeare read widely in preparation for writing this play. The wedding celebrations are developed from Chaucer's account in "The Knight's Tale," of *The Canterbury Tales*: ideas for the hunting episode could have come from here as well, and the escape of young lovers to a wood. The names of Philostrate and Egeus were taken from quite different characters in Chaucer. The quarrelling King and Queen of fairies may come from "The

Merchant's Tale" in the same collection, but the name Oberon and other details of fairy-life seem to have been found in an old romance *Huon of Bordeaux*, translated into English by Lord Berners. Puck, however, could have come from many sources—he was common in folk tales—but it may be that Reginald Scott's *Discovery of Witchcraft* (1584) was part of Shakespeare's reading here and provided numerous details; this was to be a source for the writing of *Macbeth* some ten years later.

The plays of John Lyly, especially *Gallathea, Sapho and Phao*, and *Midas* were probably more general sources for the play's transformations. In *Midas* its hero is given ass's ears as punishment from the gods for his foolishness. But the ass's head for Bottom might also have been derived from Reginald Scott, or from the popular *Golden Ass* of Apuleius, translated by William Adlington (1566), in which the hero is completely transformed into an ass. Here a young maid pays the same sort of attention to the ass-man as Titania does to the ass-headed Bottom.

Numerous passages also suggest that Ovid's *Metamorphoses,* as translated by Arthur Golding (1567), was part of Shakespeare's reading at this time. References to Cupid's gold and leaden arrows, stories of Apollo and Daphne, Philomel, Hercules and the centaurs, the death of Orpheus, Cephalus and Procris, and numerous images or personifications might all have been gathered from this one book. Certainly it was the principle source for the story of Pyramus and Thisbe, and for many details in Titania's speech about alteration in the seasons (II.i.82–117).

Yet another source was Shakespeare's own plays. From the early *Two Gentlemen of Verona* may have come the wood where the outlaws live and the contrasted pairs of lovers, with one faithless (protean) man. Witty arguments and contrasting courtly and noncourtly characters, together with an amateur performance before a courtly audience, are all found in *Love's Labor's Lost*. Echoes occur of images and phrases from other early works, some history plays, *Romeo and Juliet*, and sonnets. These debts to his own works suggest that Shakespeare wrote the *Dream* around 1595–6.

It has sometimes been supposed that the play, with its marriage celebrations and need for a considerable number of boy actors to play the fairies as well as the four female roles, was written for a celebration of an actual wedding and not for the general repertoire of the Chamberlain's Men. Queen Elizabeth (who is alluded to in II.i.161–64) attended the wedding of Elizabeth Vane to the Earl of Derby on 26 January 1595, which would make that a possible occasion. Elizabeth Carey, who married Thomas Berkeley on 19 February 1596, was the daughter of the Lord Chamberlain and therefore known to the actors' company that bore her father's and grandfather's title and enjoyed their patronage; Queen Elizabeth was her godmother. Both these weddings are at about the right time, but neither is linked in any clear way to the play; only guess-work has associated them with it.

A Midsummer Night's Dream is listed by Francis Meres in his *Palladis Tamia, Wit's Commonwealth* (1598), as one of six comedies known to have been written by Shakespeare before that time. *The Merchant of Venice*, also in Meres' list, is dated by references in its text to 1596–7, while during 1597 Shakespeare seems to have been occupied by the two *Henry IV* plays. These considerations and also stylistic indications combine to make a date of 1595–6 the most probable for composition.

*   *   *

The title-page of the first edition of *A Midsummer Night's Dream* declares that "it hath been sundry times publicly acted, by the right Honorable, the Lord Chamberlain his servants," but that is the only certain reference that has survived of the play's early life on the stage. A letter of January 1604 written by Dudley Carleton and referring to the acting of a "play of Robin Goodfellow" at court does, however, suggest a revival at that time. But compared with other of Shakespeare's plays the record is slight, and this play had to wait until a production by Madame Vestris at Covent Garden, London, in November 1840 before it was received with notable success.

In the intervening years it had been produced occasionally. In 1662, Samuel Pepys recorded in his diary that it was the "most insipid ridiculous play that ever I saw in my life." But for most of the time Shakespeare's text was used as the basis for operas and musical extravaganzas, such as *The Fairy Queen* with music by Henry Purcell or David Garrick's version, *The Fairies* of 1755, in which only six hundred lines remained of the original and only the lovers and fairies were retained. Madam Vestris' production, while restoring much of the play, was still far more spectacular than any production in Shakespeare's day. As Oberon, the actress-manager sang nine of the fourteen songs and commanded a numerous troop of female fairies. But her lead in restoring the bulk of Shakespeare's text was followed by Samuel Phelps in 1853 and Charles Kean in 1856. By now Mendelssohn's music, written for a production of a musical adaptation at Potsdam in 1843, was in general use, and seemed to dictate the tone and emphasis to most stagings for many years and decades. Max Reinhardt's productions of 1905 and 1939 were in this tradition, as was his Hollywood film of 1935.

Harley Granville-Barker was a student of Elizabethan Theatre, as well as a playwright, actor, and producer, and his production of 1914 at the Savoy

Theatre in London, while still using a fairly large cast of supernumaries, for Amazons and bridesmaids as well as fairies, had fantastic gold fairies rather than pretty and pale ones, music by Cecil Sharp in English folk traditions and not by Mendelssohn, and pillars and curtains for set (by Norman Wilkinson) in place of imitation trees and glades. Stage lighting was responsible for many bold and unusual effects, with little or no attempt at an impression of actuality. Audiences were surprised at first by Barker's direct and unsentimental presentation of the *Dream,* but it was a watershed in the stage-history of the play. Since then its popularity and frequency of performance have greatly increased, until today it is more frequently produced than ever before, and often more simply staged than in any earlier times except its own.

These two traditions remain in force in productions which are either lavish and scenic, or bare, elegant, and alert. But a further tradition was started by Peter Brook at Stratford-upon-Avon in 1970. He set the play in a white box, furnished with fittings and implements from the circus and gymnasium. The characters had a double "look," of people belonging to the world of 1970 and also of performers ready to do stunts or take part in some impersonal ritual. Visually the production was stripped of all but a very few and limited points of strong color, but it had abundant life in music, movement, speech, and imagination. Earlier productions had offered various "new interpretations": lovers who had shouted and fought like children, fairies who were dark and potentially violent, moonlight which transfomed prettiness into mystery, and bushes into bears. But Brook encouraged actors to make the play "their own." In one sense the magic was all real: it was what worked for the performers in the stripped-for-action stage-world which the director had chosen for them.

Disorientation (as in a dream), amazement, violence, self-doubt, discovery, and unaffected pleasure and joy have become more frequent in performance of the *Dream* as the play has become a dreamscape peopled by creatures of the actors' fantasies. *A Midsummer Night's Dream* is no longer a more or less innovative exercise in old-fashioned theatricality. It seems to have a life of its own, offering a wide range of challenges to actors. It can spin from a director's hands like a universe new-made and animated by present-day concerns.

Introduction to Commentary

During the spring and early summer of 1989 John Hirsch and I met at his home several times a week to tape-record this commentary. The room we sat in overlooked one of Toronto's beautiful ravines and we were able to watch the process of change from early spring to full summer green. Sadly, over this time John's physical condition deteriorated, and with it his ability to concentrate; but he never lost his love of a good argument, especially when the subject was Shakespeare. Certainly he was well prepared to discuss *A Midsummer Night's Dream*. John died on August 1, 1989, before we had finished going through Act V. Fortunately, however, as we discussed the earlier acts he had referred to the play's end, giving me enough material to work with. What follows here and in the commentary are more or less verbatim comments by John, with, I hope, judicious editing. Aside from the examples from productions by Peter Hall and Peter Brook, little was added to what John had to say.

I

I [John speaking] have done the play three times,[1] and each time my interest has been different because the text is forever open to interpretation. The fascinating thing is to what extent you can interpret before you turn the piece, the text, into something other than what it is. I'm fully aware that when I use words and phrases such as "subjective," "highly open to interpretation," "absolute value of the text," and the "absolute meaning of the text" we are in very dangerous waters, but whatever I say is said with a certain understanding that there is an indefinable Platonic constant about the text. The best possible way is to go back to the words and get down to a perhaps simplistic attitude towards it: I mean just the narrative, what I want the audience to grasp. There is the word "moon," but the whole idea about the moon is extraordinarily potent, and the connotations are certainly very much Shakespeare's. But still there is the word, and I have to investigate what that word could have meant to him and what it does in the play as a whole, and beyond that what that word means to me, quite apart from Shakespeare, or *A Midsummer Night's Dream*, or whatever—what are the connotations that arise when I hear "the moon"? So it's a combination of trying to investigate what these words must have meant to him, and what they mean to me, what these ideas mean to me—the director's interpretation is highly personal.

What are the "Platonic" constants? There was a time when *A Midsummer Night's Dream* was looked on as a fairy tale for children and that is the most obvious and most simplistic way of looking at the play. And indeed this is important because there is an innocence to the story, almost a folk element, and the narrative itself provides us with the entertainment. In the nineteenth century the play was seen only on that level, the fairy-tale level, and the play became an excuse for a romantic—I wanted to say "baroque"—extravaganza with Mendelssohn music, and elaborate sets and costumes. This was a sign of the times, a reflection of what they wanted to get out of it.

It's curious that after having gone through the whole Jan Kott view of the play,[2] we are moving back to an extraordinarily baroque interpretation of it, where most directors are using the play, as one did say, as a kind of trampoline for his ideas. So in a strange way, today we are back in the nineteenth century: the play is not investigated, and is denied a seriousness and richness and a thematic, mythological, human level which to me are the ongoing attractions of it.

We're going through a period when the productions are more interested in, or demonstrate, the imagination of the director and the set designer rather than a real inward journey towards the heart of the play—which is a fascinating journey, a process, but without any promise of arriving at the meaning. This fascinates me especially about *A Midsummer Night's Dream* and *The Tempest* because they are plays having to do with mythology, and at the heart of them is a brilliant, impenetrable ambiguity that constantly fascinates and lures you like a siren's song, captures you but never reveals totally what you are looking for: the meaning of the play. In productions of today there is a rejection of meaning, an arrogant rejection in many instances, apparent when I read reviews and directors' introductions.

I'm interested in these plays because they are incredibly rich—rich in archetypal relationships, rich because of the language—and because the plays tell me so much about myself at a given time through the way in which I try to solve the mystery, so I'm solving my own mystery in a sense.

Naturally, any good production will reflect the preoccupations of the times even when you are not focusing on these matters—unless the production is mindless, thoughtless, unimaginative, not serious. What is essential is to make connections—as in E.M. Forster's "only connect"[3]—one wants to use this piece of work because one believes that it speaks to an audience. The issue is how it speaks to the audience and what you believe will be of benefit to them when they are witnessing the play, and this very much depends on the people who are performing it.

When I first directed *A Midsummer Night's Dream* I was fascinated by the narrative and the fun of it, and I took a sort of light-hearted approach which now kind of turns my stomach because I think, how could one be so blind and not see what one was dealing with; but I was in my early twenties and had just learned to speak English. It was an appropriate level for a beginner: emphasizing the narrative and the humor of it, and the music of it. But as I went along, and did the play at Stratford [1968], I had read Kott and had lived a bit, and read a bit, and all that went into the production; and it was in the sixties, so it was a fairly sensuous, sexual exploration of the play—an element that is in it. When I did the play in Minneapolis [1972] this darker element of the play, this kind of a disturbing eroticism, was even more present in my mind, and in the times.

The second production at Stratford [1984] contained all those elements, but there was an added interest, and that had to do with Jung, and with a feminist approach; it was more philosophically mature because I discovered those elements [of psychology, feminism] in the play. It is this richness that one wants to convey to an audience without them thinking about it, without stopping their enjoyment.

There are two main means of doing this: the actors—their interpretation of the play—and the visual aspect; and the sensual aspects, the aural aspects. You have to have a very clear idea of what you are going to do visually because there is a set designer who needs four or five weeks to do it. So you have to make decisions and some of these decisions trap you, because in a sense what occurs in the direction of a play is a process of discovery. You don't know what you are dealing with, however much you have worked things out on paper and thought about it, until you are actually there. So it's a judicious working between a very strong concept—which you have to have because there is so little time—and allowing the actors and the designer, and yourself, to discover exactly what you're dealing with, and it is absolutely impossible to predetermine all that. You have to have a direction, a road to follow, but God help you if you don't take the attractive byway that presents itself. The great pleasure of working with actors is—if you work with intelligent actors—what they bring and what they discover; and to some extent they change things, and it's desirable that things should change in the process.

II

It is crucial how you cast a play because that's when you lock in your concept of it and of the characters. If you cast Puck as a girl or as a boy you have made certain decisions that have nothing to do with the lines or the play. But there is a relationship between Oberon and Puck: there is a sexuality in that relationship which is important, a sexuality that is very ambiguous. So such decisions are major.

I have used doubling twice [for Theseus/Oberon, Hippolyta/Titania] because what's important for me is to create a unity for the production—which is very difficult to do because of the fragmentary nature of the piece—and I am forever looking at the connections. To describe this play I use the metaphor of a braided bread: each piece is a part of it but sort of separate also. My investigation of the play forever has been what are the connections, how does this thing hang together, what are the resonances that feed each other? How does it work?

And I came to the conclusion that the whole fairyland is a subconscious statement of the main themes of the play. As in all of Shakespeare's plays, when you move into the forest there is a kind of liberation—the rule of the instinct, of sexuality, of no limit. And I believe that Titania and Oberon are simply the subconscious playing out of Hippolyta and Theseus, but you have to set that up and take it through the whole play. Similarly, the play-within-the-play is a parody of lovers and love, and the power of illusion. The doubling is thematic, part of the dazzling thematic richness.

III

I always have trouble remembering Lysander's and Demetrius' names. But conveying the difference between them is the director's job, and is done in casting. Lysander is the more romantic of the lovers and Demetrius is a kind of a jock: a macho guy, an opportunist in a three-piece suit, a Harvard Business management type. This reflects on the two girls because Helena is a very bright, not too good-looking girl, and she is absolutely besotted by this Bay Street[4] guy who is very much into getting the blondest, the most beautiful, yuppie kind of girl. These are the kinds of images a director must give actors, contemporary images they understand. Establishing this context is the first step.

Lysander is more a poet, his language is more poetic; the only thing is that Hermia is a really tough girl who has been acting this sugar and cream and pink feminine thing which is not really what she is. Helena, on the other hand, is very feminine, except she hasn't the looks and she's cursed with that height, and knowing that she will never get the man she wants, because why would this gorgeous up-and-coming young lawyer with a Mercedes want her. And this is marvellously stated in the quartet of mad lovers, mad because they are in the forest, obviously.

Theseus and Hippolyta learn something about themselves and their relationship, and you cannot convey it without the forest. Or, because they are older, we see what's below the formal presence of Theseus and Hippolyta; and underneath is a wild, unbridled *liason dangereuse*. I always say to the actors who play Titania and Oberon: "You have been together for two thousand years, what's left? How can you get your kicks except by creating these situations? And she gets this Indian boy and that's really the necessary irritant, it's the 'cap on the toothpaste' thing; you've got to find something to fight about, to keep this relationship dynamic." That's one element of it. The other is the incredible voyeurism of Oberon, which again comes from the fact that there is nothing left to be done in this relationship, so it is loaded in that way. But the relationship of Titania and Oberon is a revelation of that of Hippolyta and Theseus—in a sense they work out their problem in the forest in the persons of Titania and Oberon. Like Hippolyta, Titania is a balanced person; Oberon, like Theseus, is not. If the roles of the two women and two men are doubled, this aspect of Hippolyta—Jung's "eternal feminine"—is conveyed. It is the men who must change.

It is crucial to set up the male dominance theme from the start. That is the core of this play. This is why it's important, as far as I'm concerned, that there is some kind of a clue, some kind of a context which is set up visually and theatrically to indicate that these Amazons serve Diana, the moon goddess, and they are dealing with a highly patriarchal, macho society which has no room for any of the feminine virtues, the humane qualities. The connotations of Athens and Theseus and Hippolyta have to be conveyed to a modern audience.

You have to convey the idea that this is a city ruled by men. Not a civilized place but a brutal, patriarchal, Mars-governed society. This is a granite place, it does not give; there is the subjugation of the feminine element, the subjugation of the human. And it is legalistic: "We are here to adhere to the law and there is no argument; you can cry, you can do whatever you want, this is how it is, and don't annoy me with your human problems and don't try to appeal to my humanity, my emotions." But at the end, the ruler of this city, Theseus, is going to come out and talk about imagination and illusion and love. This is why it is important to connect these things.

The play begins with "Now," which can imply antecedent action establishing a context for the initial dialogue and introducing themes. We know from what Theseus says to Hippolyta that he has defeated her in battle [I.i.16–17], so a prelude might be added which presents a brutal, physical fight between the men and the women, with the female Amazons against Theseus's men. Perhaps she is almost winning, on the verge of defeating Theseus, and the way he escapes is by having two men on the balcony throw a huge net and capture her. Then they lift her on four spears like a captive animal. This annihilates the will to fight in the rest of the Amazons and they are chased out and captured; then Hippolyta is freed and the play begins. If this is done, a leap in time must be conveyed by a blackout because the first scene is in the court.

Hippolyta's reluctance at the beginning can be conveyed by having her stand apart from the rest of them; thus Theseus has to go up to her, take the initiative. As an Amazon, Hippolyta is associated with Diana and the moon. To convey the qualities she embodies she might wear a magic crystal around her neck which she constantly touches.[5] This charm can be used as the means by which she contacts the moon and by which the audience is reminded of her relationship to it.

IV

Who are the mechanicals? How do they look? What is the age difference? The actors should ask themselves what has happened before I.ii to bring these men together. How were they recruited? How long did it take? How much persuasion was necessary? I see Quince as an older man who has been scribbling all his life; he has written an epic poem and some lyrics, sonnets, and he has attempted this play. And he reads: he has one or two books—certainly one on mythology, Ovid's *Metamorphoses*. There is something of an amateur scholar about him; he's interested in learning. He is obviously fascinated by the theatre and is glad of this opportunity to produce his play.

Snug the joiner (Lion) is like Bert Lahr in *The Wizard of Oz:* a big, dopey guy, very pleasant, who has been recruited, who brings a huge submarine sandwich and a bottle of beer. He is pleasant but doesn't really know what is going on.

Bottom the weaver is an amateur actor—whenever there is a show, a musical, a tragedy, whatever, he is ready to do it. And like so many in little theatre, he thinks he knows better than anybody else, he is the expert, and he has a good-sized ego. He does not shut up because he is so full of himself, not in a malicious and evil way like professional actors, but simply because he knows that whatever he has to contribute is invaluable because he has experience. He knows how to conduct a rehearsal because he has been in many plays, and has worked with many lousy directors, and he will tell this to everyone around. And he has an active imagination—why? because his job is sedentary, and solitary, and repetitious. While he works there are things going on in his head; he has a marvelous imagination. That he is a weaver is connected with how he acts: he is a dreamer, weaving his own dreams, especially of being an actor. The enthusiasm is created by Bottom, because Quince is quiet and rather scholarly and careful, he is not an artist really; he doesn't have the imagination or the ability to make others enthusiastic—certainly he doesn't have a chance when Bottom is around.

The actor who plays Bottom must be a very good one; he must be able to portray a man who is charming, lovable, agile, innocent. Without this quality of innocence the play does not work (note his sense of wonder when he wakes up). He has to be an innocent, like all great actors are—the child-like quality must be predominant, and the imagination. Bottom is an artist. He may not be a great actor, but he has imagination, and he has skill, which the rest of them do not. Bottom represents the necessary mixture of the feminine—the imaginative, the instinctive—and the masculine desire to control the situation in order to be oneself.

Flute the bellows-mender (Thisbe) is a young boy who is absolutely besotted with Bottom. He watches his every move to see how it is done. In every cast there is one of these. He is full of energy and of the wonder of what is to come.

Snout the Tinker has been recruited by Quince; they go to the same pub and Quince has asked him, "Would you like to be in our play?" and Snout has said, "Are you kidding?" and Quince has told him he can make some money, so he has agreed.

Starveling the tailor is a neat, sweet man; and what do tailors do? They sit together and work, and dream, and they tell stories to one another. How does he sit? What does he sit on? Did he bring his own chair, the cushion he sits on all day? Did he bring his work; if so, he is sewing all the time he is there.

V

To create the play's sense of urgency and movement it should be staged so that before one person exits, the next is already on. The action rushes forward in keeping with the madness it's about. There is a relentless, frenetic quality—a brutality. There are only slight moments of lyricism that permit a brief release. The set should not be cluttered up with furniture or scenery that would inhibit the forward movement Shakespeare intends. The few props the characters bring on with them and their actions are sufficient to give life to the scene and create a world for the audience to perceive. A totally empty

Elizabethan stage is the best way to deal with the play because of the tremendous speed of events; anything that impedes the rush of the action lessens the play, its quality of madness. Everything we have to see is conveyed by the language.

This is not a children's play; it is a work of great complexity and a director must decide how to strike a balance between comedy, enjoyment, and the darker, more thematic elements. The actors and director must take an approach that does not encourage the audience to think this is going to be a fun comedy and they can sit back and enjoy themselves without becoming involved. They must be brought to see that it has a connection with reality, with them as human beings.

THREE PRODUCTIONS

As John Hirsch says, each director interprets the play in his or her own way, and according to the times. To give a sense of various possibilities for staging *A Midsummer Night's Dream*, John's commentary, which is based especially on his 1984 production, is supplemented with examples from the well-known, and very different, productions by Peter Hall (1959, 1962) and Peter Brook (1970). The diverse conceptions of these three directors are apparent in the critics' descriptions of the sets and costumes.

According to Roger Warren, Hirsch's 1984 Stratford, Ontario, production was beautiful. Designer Desmond Heeley "completely transformed" the Festival theatre's "stark platform" into a forest in a way that "subtly mirrored the text: the stage and balcony were filled almost from floor to roof with tall, slender saplings; but the brown leaves on those midsummer trees perfectly reflected the confusion of the seasons which Titania describes and which in turn reflects the chaotic relationships in both the fairy kingdom and the mortal world." The "fairies' costumes were variations on the Elizabethan styles worn by the mortals, but in addition Oberon's branched head-dress carried the suggestion of a tree-spirit" (Warren 1987, pp. 182–83).

For Peter Hall's 1959 Royal Shakespeare Company production at Stratford-upon-Avon, the set by Lila de Nobili suggested the "great chamber" (III.i.47–48) of an Elizabethan manor house. The permanent set of unpainted wood contained a "gallery reached by two great staircases upon which fairies and lovers could chase each other." In the wood scenes, the gallery became a "rustic bridge" and "the painted backcloth depicting an Elizabethan interior was lit from behind so that it became transparent, and a grove of saplings was visible above the steps" (Brown 1960, p. 143). To supplement these, "bushes in pots and branches [were] brought on by the actors."

"A curtained-off recess, reminiscent of the Elizabethan theater's inner stage, [served as] Titania's bower." The stage was strewn with rushes (Byrne, p. 155). In 1962, when the production was remounted at Stratford, the set was still the "balconied hall of an Elizabethan mansion...but with the wood growing up round and behind the staircases and balconies" (Trewin, p. 514). When the production moved to London's Aldwych Theatre in 1963, "the staircases and balcony were replaced by a large empty hall in warm red... brick. The entire wood was moved into this hall on a platform, complete with a large tree and flowering bushes" (Warren 1983, p. 47).

Hall's Oberon and Titania wore Elizabethan court costumes, some copied from Hilliard miniatures (Brown 1960, p. 143), "but the misty fabric of which these were made also suggested the cobwebs, dew and gossamer of the wood" (Warren 1983, p. 50). The fairies were costumed in "shimmering greens, silvers and golds: but they were also barefoot, touslehaired, wild-eyed, slightly tattered in appearance" and wore pixie's ears (Addenbrooke, p.116). Hall described the fairies as "sexy and wicked and kinky...they aren't pretty creatures hopping about: they have animal senses. I've always tried... to make them earthy, so that they're more sensual than the mortals."[6]

For Peter Brook's innovative 1970 RSC production, Sally Jacobs designed a set of three white walls "rising to about eighteen feet and topped by a practical gallery from which actors not on stage were constantly surveying those who were, and contributing where necessary to the mechanics of the staging. Two upstage doors...provided the only access at stage level, but there were ladders at the downstage end of both side walls, and trapezes slung from the flies could lower and raise Oberon, Puck, Titania and the four fairies" (Thomson, pp.125–26). The stage floor was covered in soft white matting, and the only furniture was four white cushions. The play began with the white set and bright white light. The woods were created by wire coils suspended from above from fishing rods held by the fairies. Exotic music was created by zithers, guitars, and bongos, and the characters often shifted to song at moments of high emotion; as well, drums punctuated the dialogue and thunder sheets rolled in full view of the audience; tree coils produced metallic music as they moved and settled.[7]

"Demetrius and Lysander wore smocks of smudged pastel design over pressed white flannels, Helena and Hermia wore long side-slit dresses with same smudged pastel decoration. Oberon wore deep purple, Titania bright green, the Mechanicals the working clothes of British labourers in the age of austerity" (Thomson, p. 126). The fairies, in grey, were four hefty, sinister men, very masculine with long hair and mustaches.

Brook used doubling to suggest that the events in the wood represented the dark animal fantasies beneath the public front which Theseus and Hippolyta present to the world. To Brook, Theseus/Oberon has Hippolyta/Titania raped "by the crudest sex machine he can find"; Oberon's clear intention is to "degrade Titania as a woman."[8] This production took the doubling farther than others: in the forest Philostrate became Puck, Egeus became Quince, and Theseus's courtiers became the fairies. The implication was that "the lovers carried with them into their dream all the familiar faces of the Athenian Court" (Thomson, p. 126).

NOTES

1. At Stratford, Ontario, in 1968, at Minneapolis in 1972, and again at Stratford in 1984.
2. See Jan Kott, *Shakespeare Our Contemporary*, tr. Boleslaw Taborski (London: Methuen, 1966).
3. *Howard's End* (London: Edward Arnold, 1910, 1973), pp. 183–84.
4. Bay Street in Toronto is the equivalent of New York's Wall Street, or the City in London.
5. In Hirsch's 1968 production, Hippolyta carried a rose, which she gave to Hermia as she left the stage in the first scene. (For a description of this staging see Philip McGuire, *Speechless Dialect*, pp. 5–7.)
6. Addenbrooke, quoting an interview with Hall by Gordon Gow in *Films and Filming*, September, 1969.
7. See Addenbrooke, p. 167; Barber; Dukore, pp. 93–94.
8. Interview in *Plays and Players,* October 1970.

REFERENCES AND ABBREVIATIONS

Addenbrooke	David Addenbrooke, *The Royal Shakespeare Company: The Peter Hall Years* (London: William Kimber, 1974).
Barber	John Barber, *Daily Telegraph*, 28 August 1970.
Beauman	Sally Beauman, *The Royal Shakespeare Company: A History of Ten Decades*, (Oxford, New York, Toronto, Melbourne: Oxford UP, 1982).
Brown 1960	J.R. Brown, "Three Adaptations," *Shakespeare Survey* 13 (1960): 137–45.
Brown 1971	J.R. Brown, "Free Shakespeare," *Shakespeare Survey* 24 (1971): 127–35.

Byrne	M. St. Clare Byrne, "Shakespeare at The Old Vic, 1958–59 and Stratford-upon-Avon, 1959," *Shakespeare Quarterly* 10 (1959): 544–67.
A. Dawson	Anthony Dawson, *Watching Shakespeare: A Playgoers' Guide* (London: Macmillan, 1988).
H. Dawson	Helen Dawson, *The Observer*, 30 August 1970.
Dukore	Bernard F. Dukore, untitled review in *Educational Theatre Journal* 23 (1971): 93–94.
Evans	Gareth Lloyd Evans, *Shakespeare II* 1587–1598 (Edinburgh: Oliver and Boyd, 1969).
Fiddick	Peter Fiddick, *The Guardian*, 28 August 1970.
Marcus	Frank Marcus, *Sunday Telegraph*, 30 August 1970.
McGuire 1985	Philip C. McGuire, *Speechless Dialect: Shakespeare's Open Silences* (Berkeley, Los Angeles, London: U of California P, 1985).
McGuire 1989	—-, "Egeus and the Implications of Silence," in *Shakespeare and the Sense of Performance*, ed. Warren and Ruth Thompson (Newark: U of Delaware P; London and Toronto: Assoc. UP, 1989), pp. 103–15.
Percival	John Percival, *Plays and Players* 10 (August 1963), p. 48.
Roberts	Peter Roberts, *Plays and Players* 18 (October 1970).
Selbourne	David Selbourne, *The Making Of "A Midsummer Night's Dream": An eyewitness account of Peter Brook's production from first rehearsal to first night* (London: Methuen, 1982).
Speaight	Robert Speaight, "Shakespeare in Britain," *Shakespeare Quarterly* 21 (1970): 439–49.
Styan	J. L. Styan, *The Shakespeare Revolution: Criticism and Performance in the Twentieth Century* (London, New York, Melbourne: Cambridge UP, 1977).
Thomson	Peter Thomson, "A Necessary Theatre: The Royal Shakespeare Season 1970 Reviewed," *Shakespeare Survey* 24 (1971): 117–28.
Trewin	J.C. Trewin, "The Old Vic and Stratford-upon-Avon 1961–1962," *Shakespeare Quarterly* 13 (1962): 514–15.
Wardle	Irving Wardle, *The Times*, 28 August 1970.
Warren 1983	Roger Warren, *"A Midsummer Night's Dream": Text and Performance* (Macmillan, 1983).
Warren 1987	—-, "The John Hirsch Years," *Shakespeare Survey* 39 (1987): 179–90.

CHARACTERS

THESEUS, Duke of Athens

EGEUS, father to Hermia

LYSANDER
DEMETRIUS } in love with Hermia

PHILOSTRATE, Master of the Revels to Theseus

HIPPOLYTA, Queen of the Amazons, betrothed to Theseus

HERMIA, daughter to Egeus, in love with Lysander

HELENA, in love with Demetrius

Attendants on Theseus and Hippolyta

PETER QUINCE, a carpenter; Prologue in *Pyramus and Thisbe*

SNUG, a joiner; Lion in *Pyramus and Thisbe*

NICK BOTTOM, a weaver; Pyramus in *Pyramus and Thisbe*

FRANCIS FLUTE, a bellows mender; Thisbe in *Pyramus and Thisbe*

TOM SNOUT, a tinker; Wall in *Pyramus and Thisbe*

ROBIN STARVELING, a tailor; Moonshine in *Pyramus and Thisbe*

OBERON, King of the Fairies

PUCK, or Robin Goodfellow

TITANIA, Queen of the Fairies

PEASEBLOSSOM
COBWEB
MUSTARDSEED
MOTH } fairies attending Titania

Other Fairies attending their King and Queen

Scene: Athens, and a wood near it

ACT I

Scene i.   *Enter* Theseus, Hippolyta, [Philostrate,] *with others.*

Theseus   Now, fair Hippolyta, our nuptial hour
  Draws on apace. Four happy days bring in
  Another moon — but O, methinks how slow
  This old moon wanes! She lingers° my desires,
  Like to a stepdame or a dowager,   5
  Long withering° out a young man's revenue.°

Hippolyta   Four° days will quickly steep° themselves in night,
  Four nights will quickly dream away the time,
  And then the moon, like to a silver bow
  New-bent in heaven, shall behold the night   10
  Of our solemnities.°

Theseus   Go Philostrate,
  Stir up the Athenian youth to merriments,°
  Awake the pert° and nimble spirit of mirth.
  Turn melancholy forth to funerals;
  The pale companion° is not for our pomp.°   15

               [*Exit* Philostrate.]

  Hippolyta, I wooed thee with my sword°,
  And won thy love, doing thee injuries;
  But I will wed thee in another key,
  With pomp, with triumph,° and with reveling.

     Enter Egeus *and his daughter* Hermia, *and*
       Lysander *and* Demetrius.

Egeus   Happy be Theseus, our renownèd Duke!   20

Theseus   Thanks, good Egeus. What's the news with thee?

Egeus   Full of vexation° come I, with complaint
  Against my child, my daughter Hermia.
  Stand forth, Demetrius. My noble lord,
  This man hath my consent to marry her.   25
  Stand forth, Lysander. And, my gracious Duke,

Stage Directions: The stage fills with the two leaders and their followers, uneasy with each other. Brook's production began with the whole company swooping down on stage in long white capes; "Flinging off their capes, the actors suddenly became the characters, dressed in brilliant colours against the pure white background." (A. Dawson, p. 23)

1-6 Theseus' first words convey urgency; and if there is a prologue showing Hippolyta's defeat (see introduction) the "now" will have special meaning for her. For his part, Theseus speaks with the courtier-audience in mind; they know he nearly lost the fight. Theseus is impatient, anxious about bringing this marriage to pass. There is a kind of put-down of the moon by him: it is not Diana, the changing, the goddess, the powerful, but the "old" moon that "wanes." The importance of transformation and change is introduced at the start. From the first words there is a time frame for the action.

draws out, puts off

wastes;   i.e., inheritance
(the action of the play lasts only two days); soak, drown

7-11 Unlike Theseus, Hippolyta is in no hurry, and her poetic description of the moon is in contrast to Theseus' attitude. Her moon/bow image (ll. 9-10) is likely an allusion to the goddess Diana, the huntress. As an Amazon, Hippolyta is connected with the cosmos via Diana, who is goddess of the moon and the hunt. As well, the hunt reference anticipates the hunting scene in which both Theseus and Hippolyta participate (IV.i). In the 1959 Hall production, Hippolyta (Stephanie Bidmead) "leer[ed] knowingly as she [spoke] to her intended husband of 'the night of our solemnities'" (Brown, 1960, p.144).

nuptials

entertainments
lively

(contemptuous)   grand and proud procession

(he captured her in battle)

11-15 Theseus' imperatives convey his desire to get this wedding done. "Turn melancholy forth to funerals" (14) might be a reference to Hippolyta's state: she is not eager; she is standing apart, not participating in the arrangements for this enforced wedding. Perhaps he moves to embrace her, and she draws back.

public festivity, victory parade

16-19 Theseus is uncomfortable and disturbed because he has to assert his authority and he also wants to win over Hippolyta. Can he dominate her? His followers have spears and swords, but she has nearly defeated him. Possibly Hippolyta is visibly reluctant; she does not reply to him. If she is not next to Theseus, but somewhere off on the periphery, she

grief, distress

This man hath bewitched the bosom of my child.
Thou, thou, Lysander; thou hast given her rhymes,
And interchanged love-tokens with my child.
Thou hast by moonlight at her window sung,   30
With feigning° voice, verses of feigning° love,
And stol'n the impression of her fantasy°
With bracelets of thy hair, rings, gauds,° conceits,°
Knacks,° trifles, nosegays, sweetmeats — messengers
Of strong prevailment° in unhardened youth.   35
With cunning hast thou filched my daughter's heart,
Turned her obedience, which is due to me,
To stubborn harshness.° And, my gracious Duke,
Be it so° she will not here before your Grace
Consent to marry with Demetrius,   40
I beg the ancient privilege of Athens:
As she is mine, I may dispose of her,
Which shall be either to this gentleman
Or to her death, according to our law
Immediately° provided° in that case.   45

THESEUS   What say you, Hermia? Be advised, fair maid.
To you your father should be as a god,
One that composed° your beauties; yea, and one
To whom you are but as a form in wax
By him imprinted, and within his power   50
To leave the figure or disfigure it.
Demetrius is a worthy gentleman.

HERMIA   So is Lysander.

THESEUS   In himself he is;
But in this kind,° wanting your father's voice,°
The other must be held the worthier.   55

HERMIA   I would my father looked but with my eyes.

THESEUS   Rather your eyes must with his judgement look.

HERMIA   I do entreat your Grace to pardon me.
I know not by what power I am made bold,
Nor how it may concern° my modesty   60
In such a presence here to plead my thoughts;
But I beseech your Grace that I may know

acquires a greater strength than if she were standing next to him.

In Brook's production, "Theseus [Alan Howard] and Hippolyta [Sara Kestelman] spoke their opening lines to the audience as they knelt ritualistically on cushions" (Styan, p.231). Brook's version conveyed gravity, but not reluctance on Hippolyta's part; there was no sense of conflict between Hippolyta and Theseus (A. Dawson, p.23).

With the entrance of Egeus and the others, Hippolyta suddenly realizes the world she is about to marry into. Still she does not say anything, but her expression is important.

Veiled, soft   deceitful (with pun on "faining" = affectionate, desirous)

surreptitiously captured her imagination

trinkets   fanciful gifts

knick-knacks

power to influence

discord, offensiveness

if so be

20-26 The entrance of Egeus and Hermia might be signalled by her screaming as she is being dragged on by her father accompanied by a banging of doors and attempts to prevent him from entering. This is a moment of disorder because he has no appointment and should not just barge into the court. Egeus enters first, fuming and dragging Hermia almost by her hair, a male insisting on his rights without any reference to the female's wishes. Conversation begins formally, coolly: this is not an enthusiastic greeting. Theseus really wants to ask Egeus why he is interrupting, who allowed him in.

expressly, without appeal stipulated (legal term)

Egeus, "full of vexation" (l. 22), explodes the tension that has built through the scene. The repetition of "my" suggests that to him his daughter is nothing but an object to be disposed of however he wants. Demetrius and Lysander react differently: perhaps Demetrius just stands there, looking askance at this barbaric behaviour; Lysander might move to protect Hermia from her angry father and must be restrained. The two men are asked to "stand forth" (ll. 24,26) and are defined by Egeus, helping to fix them in the audience's minds. Perhaps Demetrius stands close to Egeus—right from the start they are allies— whereas Lysander stands apart.

framed (in begetting)

in a matter of this nature vote

28-45 Egeus wants an immediate solution. These men have no patience, they do not negotiate. It is worth asking what happened before father and daughter came to Theseus; how long has this been going on? What kind of yelling and screaming went on at home? Did he beat her? Throw dishes at her? Did she do the same? It is clear he would rather see her dead than follow her inclinations. To convey Egeus' dominance, Hermia might be pushed to the floor by him and when she tries to get up he pushes

befit

The worst that may befall me in this case,°
If I refuse to wed Demetrius.

THESEUS   Either to die the death,° or to abjure   65
Forever the society of men.
Therefore, fair Hermia, question your desires;
Know of° your youth, examine well your blood,°
Whether, if you yield not to your father's choice,
You can endure the livery° of a nun,   70
For aye to be in shady cloister mewed,°
To live a barren sister all your life,
Chanting faint hymns to the cold fruitless moon.°
Thrice-blessed they that master so their blood,
To undergo such maiden pilgrimage;   75
But earthlier happy° is the rose distilled,°
Than that which, withering on the virgin thorn,
Grows, lives, and dies in single° blessedness.

HERMIA   So will I grow, so live, so die, my lord,
Ere I will yield my virgin patent° up   80
Unto his lordship, whose unwishèd yoke
My soul consents not to give sovereignty.

THESEUS   Take time to pause, and by the next new moon —
The sealing day betwixt my love and me,
For everlasting bond of fellowship —   85
Upon that day either prepare to die
For disobedience to your father's will,
Or else to wed Demetrius, as he would,°
Or on Diana's altar to protest°
For aye austerity and single life.   90

DEMETRIUS   Relent, sweet Hermia: and Lysander yield
Thy crazèd° title to my certain right.

LYSANDER   You have her father's love, Demetrius,
Let me have Hermia's — do you marry him.

EGEUS   Scornful Lysander! True, he hath my love,   95
And what is mine my love shall render him.
And she is mine, and all my right of her
I do estate° unto Demetrius.

LYSANDER   I am, my lord, as well derived° as he,

her down again. Lysander perhaps moves to intervene and someone grabs him and stops him while Demetrius does his best to avoid becoming involved, letting Egeus do all the work because that way he will not be implicated and alienate himself from Hermia.

46-52 Theseus knows he has to do more than just enforce the law if he is to gain Hippolyta's respect. He has been a warrior and conquered her; now he must display other qualities to attract this rebellious, dignified strong woman. Unfortunately for him it is just the wrong complaint: it is Theseus' luck to have a rebellious daughter and a half-mad father who insists on her marrying somebody she does not want. There is much to suggest that Hippolyta is similarly reluctant to marry Theseus.

53-64 As the scene progresses, possibly Hermia feels Hippolyta's power, is given courage by it, and begins to drift towards her. Nothing is said, but she moves as if drawn by a magnet towards Hippolyta, towards Diana: the influence of the moon. As Hermia rebels and begins to oppose her father and Theseus, Hippolyta moves closer into the circle. Seeing this, Theseus becomes even more upset. When Hermia finally speaks it is like three gunshots, an explosion of resistance (l. 53).

If Theseus gave vent to his feelings, he would slap her. Instead he becomes legalistic, and reinforces, albeit in a friendly way, the patriarchal quality of the Athenian society (ll. 53-55). But again Hermia has a quick answer (l. 56); the effect is like a clanging of swords. Theseus' strong response (l. 57) causes Hermia to change her approach; until now she has been just a cheeky, rebellious girl, lacking in manners and respect. Perhaps Hermia and Hippolyta make eye contact just before Hermia refers to the "power" (l. 59). Hermia's desire to know the worst (ll. 63-64) suggests that until now Hermia has not taken her father's threats seriously.

65-90 Theseus must tell her the law, but he makes a tactical error in describing the alternatives: Hippolyta is a votaress of Diana, yet he speaks negatively of the moon. For the Amazon Hippolyta and the goddess Diana, being a virgin and serving the moon is commendable. This again gives Hippolyta the opportunity for signs of unease. Theseus does not speak just to Hermia, but to Hippolyta as well, and to everyone else. This is a political, public court

---

Marginal glosses:

(legal term)

be put to death

consider   feelings, passions

habit
confined, caged

i.e., Diana, goddess of chastity

happier on earth   i.e.,
    plucked and distilled for
    perfume
i.e., unmarried

rights, privilege

wishes, requires
vow

flawed, unsound

settle upon

of as good descent

As well possessed;° my love is more than his;   100
My fortunes every way as fairly ranked
(If not with vantage)° as Demetrius';
And, which is more than all these boasts can be,
I am beloved of beauteous Hermia.
Why should not I then prosecute° my right?   105
Demetrius, I'll avouch it to his head,°
Made love to Nedar's daughter, Helena,
And won her soul; and she, sweet lady, dotes,
Devoutly dotes, dotes in idolatry,
Upon this spotted° and inconstant man.   110

THESEUS   I must confess that I have heard so much,
And with Demetrius thought to have spoke thereof;
But, being overfull of self affairs,
My mind did lose it. But Demetrius come;
And come Egeus. You shall go with me;   115
I have some private schooling for you both.
For you, fair Hermia, look you arm° yourself
To fit your fancies to your father's will,
Or else the law of Athens yields you up —
Which by no means we may extenuate °—   120
To death, or to a vow of single life.
Come my Hippolyta: what cheer, my love?
Demetrius and Egeus, go along;
I must employ you in some business
Against° our nuptial, and confer with you   125
Of something nearly° that concerns yourselves.

EGEUS   With duty and desire we follow you.
                          Exeunt [all but LYSANDER *and* HERMIA.]
LYSANDER   How now, my love! Why is your cheek so pale?
How chance the roses there do fade so fast?

HERMIA   Belike° for want of rain, which I could well   130
Beteem° them from the tempest of my eyes.

LYSANDER   Ay me! For aught that I could ever read,
Could ever hear by tale or history,
The course of true love never did run smooth;
But either it was different in blood°—   135

HERMIA   O cross! Too high to be enthralled to low!

as rich

advantage on my side

pursue
to his face

morally stained

prepare

mitigate

in preparation for
closely

probably
grant

parentage, rank

scene. Hermia shoots back in a clarion-call for her independence, individuality (ll. 79-82). A shocked Theseus gives her the alternatives. He wants to resolve everything quickly and regain control.

91-94 The two suitors argue over Hermia, but there is no mention of love; they could be talking about possession of a cow. Finally Lysander explodes; he has been prevented, perhaps even physically, from speaking, and his anger has been building.

Theseus and Hippolyta will respond to this exchange. The situation is worsening by the minute for Theseus; people are shouting at one another, and Hippolyta's fears of this masculine, conservative, unbending, mad court are confirmed; he watches her reactions. There is comedy in how it steadily gets worse for him.

99-110 Realizing that nothing will persuade Egeus and Demetrius, Lysander turns to Theseus. He begins with the material things, but what it comes down to is "love," "beloved": mutual love (ll. 100, 104). He then pulls out his ace-in-the-hole: that Demetrius is not to be trusted because he has also courted Helena. Why has no one mentioned this so far? Is Demetrius deceitful, not to be trusted? This is the final straw for Theseus; he and the others learn he has been defending someone not worth it.

111-26 Theseus' confession indicates how he has played the scene: he has been focused on Hippolyta, and he has made a mistake. Nevertheless, the law is the law, and he repeats it. Theseus asks, "What cheer, my love?" (l. 122), perhaps because Hippolyta has turned away or looked shocked in response to his edict. If this makes him angry, he does not show it here. Instead, he turns to Demetrius and Egeus saying he wants to discuss preparations for his wedding (ll. 114-16, 123-26); but given the situation they have put him in he probably wants to scold them in private. Egeus exits like an old sheep dog (see l. 127), followed by Demetrius, totally disgraced because Lysander spoke the truth about him and Helena. As they follow Theseus out, Egeus could give Demetrius a punch; perhaps Egeus only now realizes that he interrupted Theseus when he burst into the court.

When does Hippolyta exit? The order of the exits helps to convey attitudes and relationships. If Hippolyta is last to leave, it will convey that she

LYSANDER   Or else misgraffèd° in respect of years—

HERMIA   O spite! Too old to be engaged to young!

LYSANDER   Or else it stood upon° the choice of friends—

HERMIA   O hell! To choose love by another's eyes!   140

LYSANDER   Or If there were a sympathy° in choice,
            War, death, or sickness did lay siege to it,
            Making it momentary as a sound,
            Swift as a shadow, short as any dream,
            Brief as the lightning in the collied° night,   145
            That in a spleen,° unfolds° both heaven and earth,
            And ere a man hath power to say "Behold!"
            The jaws of darkness do devour it up:
            So quick bright things come to confusion.

HERMIA   If then true lovers have been ever crossed,   150
            It stands as an edict in destiny:
            Then let us teach our trial patience,°
            Because it is a customary cross,
            As due to love as thoughts and dreams and sighs,
            Wishes, and tears, poor Fancy's° followers.   155

LYSANDER   A good persuasion.° Therefore hear me, Hermia.
            I have a widow aunt, a dowager
            Of great revenue, and she hath no child.
            From Athens is her house remote seven leagues,
            And she respects° me as her only son.   160
            There, gentle Hermia, may I marry thee,
            And to that place the sharp Athenian law
            Cannot pursue us. If thou lovest me then,
            Steal forth thy father's house tomorrow night
            And in the wood a league without° the town —   165
            Where I did meet thee once with Helena
            To do observance to a morn of May,°
            There will I stay for thee.

HERMIA   My good Lysander!
            I swear to thee, by Cupid's strongest bow,
            By his best arrow with the golden head,°   170
            By the simplicity° of Venus' doves,°
            By that which knitteth souls and prospers loves,

mismatched, misgrafted

depended on

accord

blackened (as with coal dust)
flash of anger   reveals

i.e., teach ourselves to be
patient

love's, sexual fantasy's

doctrine, argument

regards, values

outside

(May Day celebrations, in
Shakespeare's England,
involved bringing green
branches from the woods
into the town)

(Cupid was said to have two
arrows; one with a lead
head to repel love, one with
a gold to cause love)

guilelessness   (sacred to
Venus)

---

leaves at her own speed, not because
wants her to. And perhaps there is an
between Hermia and Hippolyta, maybe a
comfort, reinforcing the link established
these two women in the scene.

128-49 The large court group on the stage is now
reduced to two lovers. As soon as Hermia and
Lysander are alone, she reverts to being "feminine";
actually, she has learned to play her role in a man's
world. We have already seen what stuff she is made
of in her confrontation with Theseus. Lysander uses
the same tone as Theseus with Hippolyta; "pale" perhaps implies she is sad, like Hippolyta ("What cheer,
my love?"), or frightened by the choice she must
make.

The use of one line each—stichomythia—creates a new rhythm, contrasting with long speeches:
this exchange has a musical, rhythmic quality befitting their relationship; as well it permits a clear exposition of the problem they face. There is a reinforce-
ment of the idea that they are not free to love in
Athens' legalistic, law-bound society, an important
factor in their decision to flee.

150-55 At first Hermia moans along with Lysander
about their situation, but then she sees the positive
side: everything happening to them is a sign, proof
they are true star-crossed lovers and should accept
these trials. Hermia takes the initiative; she is a
bright, practical woman, whereas Lysander is a
Byronic moaner, a Romeo, who enjoys his suffering.
Her reference to "thoughts, dreams" and "fancy"
(ll. 154-55) foreshadows Theseus' famous speech in
Act V.

156-68 Lysander agrees with her interpretation, and
suddenly the mood shifts to Grimm's fairytales:
Hansel and Gretel are going to walk into the forest
and find this good old woman; and it is seven
leagues, a lucky number. This moves into a fairytale,
Jungian dreamworld. The "morn of May" reference
(l. 167) is characteristic of the mythological element
basic to the play. Suddenly the whole spirit lifts; there
is a juxtaposition of moods here, a shift to pizzicato.

The characterization of the old woman is brief
but complete: she is a vividly realized person (ll. 157-
60). Again we have an older woman, just as
Hippolyta is in relation to Hermia—another protective
female force. Lysander's reference to having met

And by that fire which burned the Carthage queen
When the false Troyan under sail was seen,°
By all the vows that ever men have broke   175
(In number more than ever women spoke)
In that same place thou hast appointed me,
Tomorrow truly will I meet with thee.

LYSANDER   Keep promise, love. Look, here comes Helena.

Enter HELENA.

HERMIA   God speed fair Helena! Whither away?   180

HELENA   Call you me fair? That fair again unsay.
Demetrius loves your fair.° O happy fair!°
Your eyes are lodestars° and your tongue's sweet air°
More tunable° than lark to shepherd's ear
When wheat is green, when hawthorn buds appear.   185
Sickness is catching; O, were favor° so,
Yours would I catch, fair Hermia, ere I go!
My ear should catch your voice, my eye your eye,
My tongue should catch your tongue's sweet melody.
Were the world mine, Demetrius being bated,°   190
The rest I'd give to be to you translated.°
O teach me how you look, and with what art°
You sway the motion° of Demetrius' heart!

HERMIA   I frown upon him, yet he loves me still.

HELENA   O that your frowns would teach my smiles such skill!   195

HERMIA   I give him curses, yet he gives me love.

HELENA   O that my prayers could such affection move!

HERMIA   The more I hate, the more he follows me.

HELENA   The more I love, the more he hateth me.

HERMIA   His folly, Helena, is no fault of mine.   200

HELENA   None but your beauty: would that fault were mine!

HERMIA   Take comfort: he no more shall see my face;
Lysander and myself will fly this place.
Before the time I did Lysander see,

(in the *Aeneid,* Dido watched
  Aeneas sail away and then
  cast herself on a funeral
  pyre)

Hermia with Helena where he and Hermia will now
meet (ll. 166-67) subtly conveys the move Hermia is
making from girl/daughter to woman/wife. Perhaps
Lysander kneels, holding on to her as she makes the
plans.

168-79 Hermia completes Lysander's line, suggesting her eagerness and instant agreement. Her
excitement may show in a movement around the
stage: she is active, talking to him, moving about,
turning to him at each vow, each image. They are not
two people standing facing each other; they only
come together at lines 178-79. As Hermia makes her
vows the verse becomes rhymed couplets, one of the
many occasions through the play where
Shakespeare uses the verse form to accentuate the
effect. If the actor speaks the verse well, an audience
will not be conscious of the change, but it will have a
subliminal effect.

your beauty   fortunate fair
  one
i.e., attracting Demetrius' gaze,
  and guiding him   music
melodious

looks, attractiveness

180-201 When Helena enters, where is she coming
from, where is she going, and what does she know of
the events at the court—that Demetrius declared his
love for Hermia in public? We cannot know for sure.
Possibly Helena does know and thinks her situation
is hopeless; if so, when she sees them together and
Hermia's "fair Helena" acts like a match to ignite her
frustration, off she goes, to the surprise of the other
two ("Whither away?"). Helena's laments echo
Lysander's. Now, however, he watches with a certain
degree of embarrassment, and some satisfaction as
well, because Helena refers to Hermia's beauty, and
he is the possessor of it. On the one hand he looks
like a Cheshire cat because he knows their plans and
Helena does not, but also there is his embarrassed
masculine response to the hysterical woman. Hermia
is at a loss; she bears the brunt of Helena's lament
and it is not her fault. Stichomythia again creates a
sense that the action is hurtling forward, moving
faster than they can control.

excepted
transformed
skill, magic
desire, impulse

Seemed Athens as a paradise to me.   205
O then, what graces in my love do dwell,
That he hath turned a heaven unto a hell!

LYSANDER   Helen, to you our minds we will unfold:
Tomorrow night, when Phoebe° doth behold
Her silver visage in the wat'ry glass,   210
Decking with liquid pearl the bladed grass —
A time that lovers' flights doth still° conceal—
Through Athens' gates have we devised to steal.

HERMIA   And in the wood, where often you and I
Upon faint° primrose beds were wont to lie,   215
Emptying our bosoms of their counsel sweet,
There my Lysander and myself shall meet,
And thence from Athens turn away our eyes,
To seek new friends and stranger companies.°
Farewell, sweet playfellow. Pray thou for us;   220
And good luck grant thee thy Demetrius!
Keep word, Lysander: we must starve our sight
From lovers' food,° till tomorrow deep midnight.
LYSANDER   I will my Hermia.   *Exit* HERMIA.

                    Helena adieu:
As you on him, Demetrius dote on you!   225
                                                         Exit LYSANDER.

HELENA   How happy some o'er other some° can be!
Through Athens I am thought as fair as she.
But what of that? Demetrius thinks not so:
He will not know what all but he do know.
And as he errs, doting on Hermia's eyes,   230
So I, admiring of his qualities.
Things base and vile, holding no quantity,°
Love can transpose to form and dignity;
Love looks not with the eyes, but with the mind,
And therefore is winged Cupid painted blind.   235
Nor hath Love's mind° of any judgement taste;
Wings, and no eyes, figure° unheedy haste:
And therefore is Love said to be a child,
Because in choice he is so oft beguiled.
As waggish° boys in game themselves forswear,   240

(another name of Diana, goddess of the moon)

always

pale

company of strangers

i.e., sight of each other

in comparison with others

of no fixed magnitude/having no (attracting) proportions

i.e, love values beauty by what is fancied, not by what is actually visible

symbolize

playful, merry

202-25 Hermia reveals their plans, unaware of what she is doing because she is so caught up in her own pleasure. Lysander gives the specifics; the words are from a man with a romantic streak who loves language. Here is a male whose attitude toward the moon and night is different from that of Theseus. The image of the forest (ll. 214-15) reinforces the difference between it and the city—Athens; the suggestion is that the forest is a place of freedom, where confidences can be safely shared. Hermia's "Keep word, Lysander" (l. 222) may be prompted by his attempt to kiss her; she prevents him from doing so. This further affects Helena as she sees someone being loved when she has been rejected. This moment works Helena up to her reaction to what she has heard and seen. And Lysander's last words are maddening to Helena, especially "dote" (l. 225), which suggests irrationality.

226-45 Helena is finally alone and can give vent, openly, fully. First she diagnoses her situation (to l. 231), realizing things for the first time in response to what she has just seen. The excitement of listening to this speech comes from being able to hear her discoveries as they occur. Line 242 is another reminder that Helena and Demetrius were once a couple: there is the sense that when he left Helena he gave no explanation. Only now does Helena realize that Demetrius could not explain because love is blind, there is nothing rational; something she herself goes on to prove by deciding to tell Demetrius the secret she has learned (l. 246).

So the boy Love is perjured everywhere:
For ere Demetrius looked on Hermia's eyne,°
He hailed down oaths that he was only mine;
And when this hail some heat from Hermia felt,
So he dissolved° and show'rs of oaths did melt.   245
I will go tell him of fair Hermia's flight,
Then to the wood will he tomorrow night
Pursue her; and for this intelligence°,
If I have thanks, it is a dear expense:°
But herein mean I to enrich my pain,   250
To have his sight thither and back again.   *Exit.*

Scene ii.   *Enter* QUINCE *the Carpenter, and* SNUG *the Joiner,
and* BOTTOM° *the Weaver, and* FLUTE *the Bellows Mender,
and* SNOUT *the Tinker, and* STARVELING *the Tailor.*

QUINCE   Is all our company here?

BOTTOM   You were best to call them generally,° man by man,
according to the scrip.°

QUINCE   Here is the scroll of every man's name, which is thought
fit, through all Athens, to play in our interlude° before the   5
Duke and the Duchess, on his wedding day at night.

BOTTOM   First, good Peter Quince, say what the play treats on;
then read the names of the actors, and so grow to a point.°

QUINCE   Marry, our play is *The most lamentable comedy and most
cruel death of Pyramus and Thisbe.°*   10

BOTTOM   A very good piece of work, I assure you, and a merry.
Now good Peter Quince, call forth your actors by the scroll.
Masters, spread yourselves.°

QUINCE   Answer as I call you. Nick Bottom, the weaver?

BOTTOM   Ready. Name what part I am for, and proceed.   15

QUINCE   You, Nick Bottom, are set down for Pyramus.

BOTTOM   What is Pyramus? A lover or a tyrant?

QUINCE   A lover that kills himself, most gallant, for love.

eyes (old form)

broke faith (with pun on *melt*)

news, secret information
i.e., he will begrudge even a
   "thank you"

(name of core on which a
   weaver's thread was
   wound)

(mistake for "severally", indi-
   vidually)
scrap of paper (for "script")

play

draw to a conclusion

(Shakespeare parodies atten-
   tion-grabbing titles then
   common)

i.e., stop crowding around

246-51 After a segment when the situation is diag-
nosed, action follows, as before in the Lysander-
Hermia exchange. There are several possible interpretations of the last lines. "Back again" may suggest
what Helena wants to do: get Demetrius, or his
"sight" (l. 251), back again. She may hope that when
Demetrius sees Lysander and Hermia together in the
woods he will see that his situation is hopeless and
he will return to her. Desperate, she does not care
how it will affect Lysander and Hermia; all she wants
is to get Demetrius "back again" (l. 251), a phrase
that sums up her intention. She is fantasizing about
how things will work out. More literally, she could
mean she will "enrich her pain" (l. 250) by being able
to follow Demetrius into the woods and "back again."
She runs off as the other two have done, creating
another burst of action and maintaining the play's
rhythm.

Stage Directions: After the hurtling motion of the
play up to this point, the pace slows, and different
characters appear: people who want to create Art but
are ignorant of how to do it, of how to deal with fancy
poetry, but are going to put on a play because they
want to make some money—sixpence a day for life.
In Hall's production the mechanicals' scenes were
played slowly, "not only because they were slow on
the uptake, but also to suggest that they were thinking things out. They took their play very seriously,
and were determined to work out all its problems so
as to present it as effectively as possible" (Warren
1983, p. 53).
    The place is still in the city, perhaps Quince's
carpenter shop, at lunch hour or when they have finished work for the day. And they might have brought
their lunch, eating and drinking as they plan. Peter
Brook's mechanicals "entered to a cacophony of
sawing, rasping sounds, and rehearsed in... string
vests, flat caps, work trousers and braces"
(Addenbrooke, p. 167). Before Quince speaks, he
enters alone and waits; the others come in one by
one, perhaps shaking hands in greeting. This sets up
the last person to enter—Bottom. Quince knows he
has to handle Bottom carefully, to control him, and
that it is not going to be easy; he has to ask himself,
"Do I really need this trouble? I could have someone
else do the role, and I'm going to spend fifty percent
of my time handling him; but, on the other hand,
when he gets on stage he's going to woo the audience."

BOTTOM   That will ask some tears in the true performing of it. If
    I do it, let the audience look to their eyes: I will move storms, 20
    I will condole° in some measure. To the rest: yet my chief
    humor° is for a tyrant. I could play Ercles° rarely, or a part
    to tear a cat° in, to make all split.

                        The raging rocks'°
                        And shivering shocks   25
                        Shall break the locks
                            Of prison gates;
                        And Phibbus' car°
                        Shall shine from far,
                        And make and mar   30
                            The foolish Fates.

    This was lofty. Now name the rest of the players. This is
    Ercles' vein,° a tyrant's vein. A lover is more condoling.

QUINCE   Francis Flute, the bellows mender?

FLUTE   Here, Peter Quince.   35

QUINCE   Flute, you must take Thisbe on you.

FLUTE   What is Thisbe? A wand'ring knight?°

QUINCE   It is the lady that Pyramus must love.

FLUTE   Nay, faith, let not me play a woman. I have a beard coming.

QUINCE   That's all one.° You shall play it in a mask,° and you   40
    may speak as small° as you will.

BOTTOM   An° I may hide my face, let me play Thisbe too. I'll speak
    in a monstrous little voice, "Thisne, Thisne!°" "Ah, Pyramus,
    my lover dear! Thy Thisbe dear, and lady dear!"

QUINCE   No, no. You must play Pyramus: and Flute, you Thisbe. 45

BOTTOM   Well, proceed.

QUINCE   Robin Starveling, the tailor?

STARVELING   Here, Peter Quince.

QUINCE   Robin Starveling, you must play Thisbe's mother. Tom
    Snout, the tinker?   50

SNOUT   Here, Peter Quince.

1-13 Gradually Bottom takes over. The bifurcation of authority is reflected in the rest of the company who do not know whom to listen to, and move first to one, then the other. Quince gets used to the idea that Bottom will interrupt him; he speaks and is about to go on but keeps looking at Bottom, waiting for an interruption. This echoes the conflict between Theseus and Hippolyta over how to do things; like Hippolyta, Bottom is in charge (anticipating relations between Oberon and Titania). In the Brook production Bottom (David Waller) addressed lines 11-13 to the audience, "like a music-hall comedian" (Warren 1983, p. 59). Of Paul Hardwick's Bottom in the 1962 Hall production, John Percival said, "he wants desperately to be admired, and has a certain panache; definitely a character to be laughed *with* as well as *at.*"

express grief
inclination   Hercules
rant, act violently
(Shakespeare's burlesque of a
     dramatic style of the 1580s)

chariot of Phoebus, the sun
     god

14-45 Quince thinks he has allowed Bottom to have his say and can regain control, but he is wrong. He thinks he has given Bottom the best part in the play, but Bottom asks what kind of role it is. In Bottom's imagination, all roles are possible. Quince tries to impress on Bottom that this is not an ordinary lover but one who dies for love. And Bottom is off—he's a huge ham—saying, "*If* I do it" (ll. 19-20), playing the temperamental star.

style

    When Bottom gets going here he might jump up on a work table (two horses and boards, probably uneven, which the others steady). He plays to his onstage audience, and they love it, especially Flute, who is probably taking notes. Finally Quince loses his patience, resulting in another eruption of anger (l. 45).

knight errant

it makes no difference
    (ladies used masks to pro-
    tect their complexions, and
    hide themselves from pry-
    ing gazes)
light, high-pitched
if
(a pet-name for Thisbe)

46-72 Quince pauses, waiting to see if Bottom is going to say more, prompting Bottom's "Well, proceed." Now Quince wants to get it over with; he tries to speed up assigning parts. But it slows down again with the question of how to play the Lion. Bottom intervenes, perhaps demonstrating how he could roar quietly by how he does the "dove" and "nightingale" as a lion (ll.66-68). The others are enchanted by his performance. This is another "transformation," an imitation of nature but in the way the artist, the performer, wants to do it, and we believe it because of the commitment of the artist. Quince yells at Bottom in exasperation and the rest of them might react in fear that Quince will anger him.

QUINCE   You, Pyramus' father. Myself, Thisbe's father. Snug, the
joiner; you, the lion's part. And I hope here is a play fitted.

SNUG   Have you the lion's part written? Pray you, if it be, give it
me, for I am slow of study.   55

QUINCE   You may do it extempore, for it is nothing but roaring.

BOTTOM   Let me play the lion too. I will roar that I will do any
man's heart good to hear me. I will roar that I will make the
Duke say, "Let him roar again; let him roar again."

QUINCE   An you should do it too terribly, you would fright the   60
Duchess and the ladies, that° they would shriek; and that
were enough to hang us all.

ALL   That would hang us, every mother's son.

BOTTOM   I grant you, friends, if you should fright the ladies out
of their wits, they would have no more discretion but to   65
hang us: but I will aggravate° my voice so that I will roar you°
as gently as any sucking dove;° I will roar you an 'twere° any
nightingale.

QUINCE   You can play no part but Pyramus; for Pyramus is a
sweet-faced man, a proper° man as one shall see in a   70
summer's day, a most lovely gentlemanlike man. Therefore
you must needs play Pyramus.

BOTTOM   Well, I will undertake it. What beard were I best to play
it in?

QUINCE   Why, what you will.   75

BOTTOM   I will discharge° it in either your straw-color beard,
your orange-tawny beard, your purple-in-grain° beard, or
your French-crown°-color beard, your perfit° yellow.

QUINCE   Some of your French crowns have no hair at all,° and
then you will play barefaced.° But masters, here are your   80
parts; and I am to entreat you, request you, and desire you to
con° them by to-morrow night; and meet me in the palace
wood, a mile without the town, by moonlight. There will we
rehearse, for if we meet in the city, we shall be dogged with
company and our devices° known. In the meantime I will   85
draw a bill° of properties, such as our play wants. I pray you
fail me not.

so that

(for "moderate")   roar for you
(Bottom confuses "sitting
   dove" and "sucking (wean-
   ing) lamb," both proverbial-
   ly harmless)   as if it were
handsome

perform
fast-dyed red
(a gold coin)   perfect

i.e., some heads are bald from
   the French disease (syphilis)
beardless/ without disguise/
   brazenly
study, learn

plans, contrivances
list

72-73   We hear how badly Quince needs Bottom ("must needs"); he realizes no one else can do it. In Brook's production, when Bottom was refused the role of Lion he "down[ed] tools and sulkily walk[ed] off the stage up the theatre aisle" (Barber). Bottom's acquiesence (ll. 73-74) is not a giving in to Quince's insistence. Before the line he might saunter over to the far side of the stage, perhaps to the place where Hippolyta has stood apart earlier, making it apparent that Quince is in trouble because Bottom is threatening to quit.

By this time, the rest of them have seen the genius of this protean actor so they might all look at Quince to see what he is going to do, perhaps motioning Quince to go and pacify Bottom. Perhaps Flute goes to Bottom, with tears in his eyes, pleading with him to stay. Then we get this Edwardian, Henry Irving figure agreeing to play the role. Here and at line 46 Bottom pauses after his "well," keeping them in suspense about what he will say before making his concession.

73-87   The business of the beard is true to life: this is what happens in the dressing room with the wigmaster (compare Flute at ll. 39-41). Bottom is a perfectionist, knows that a part lives in the detail. The French crowns reference (l. 79) is difficult for a modern director because no one in today's audience knows what it means. Quince might put his hand between his legs and rub and leer—use a physical action to get a laugh. And perhaps his joke falls flat, no one gets it on stage or in the audience and Quince laughs weakly, showing he has no sense of humor. Quince is anxious and we hear in his pleas the burden of his task (ll. 81-83). We learn that Quince is worried about the competition and the need for secrecy. He pleads, "fail me not" (l. 87).

BOTTOM   We will meet, and there we may rehearse most obscenely°
  and courageously. Take pains; be perfit.° Adieu.

QUINCE   At the Duke's oak we meet.   90

BOTTOM   Enough. Hold, or cut bowstrings.°   *Exeunt.*

(for "seemly")
word-perfect

keep word, or be useless (?)

88-91 Bottom again takes charge. All the others just stand there, looking at the scripts they have been given, dumbfounded at what they have agreed to do. Perhaps Snug, who is to play the Lion, tries to imitate Bottom's earlier roars and actions, conning his part. Quince's directions to meet in the forest echo Lysander's speech. His "Take pains, be perfect" (89) unnerves the others, who can barely read let alone memorize and act. Quince gives his specific directions and Bottom silences him: "Enough," getting the last word.

ACT II

Scene i.   *Enter a* FAIRY *at one door, and* ROBIN GOODFELLOW
[PUCK] *at another.*

PUCK   How now, spirit! Whither wander you?

FAIRY   Over hill, over dale,
    Thorough bush, thorough° brier,
    Over park, over pale,°
    Thorough flood, thorough fire,   5
    I do wander everywhere,
    Swifter than the moon's sphere;°
    And I serve the Fairy Queen,
    To dew her orbs° upon the green.
    The cowslips tall her pensioners° be: 10
    In their gold coats spots you see:
    Those be rubies, fairy favors;°
    In those freckles live their savors.°
    I must go seek some dewdrops here
    And hang a pearl in every cowslip's ear.   15
    Farewell, thou lob° of spirits; I'll be gone.
    Our Queen and all her elves° come here anon.

PUCK   The King doth keep his revels here tonight:
    Take heed the Queen come not within his sight.
    For Oberon is passing fell and wrath,°   20
    Because that she as her attendant hath
    A lovely boy, stol'n from an Indian king—
    She never had so sweet a changeling°—
    And jealous Oberon would have the child
    Knight of his train, to trace° the forests wild.   25
    But she perforce° withholds the lovèd boy,
    Crowns him with flowers and makes him all her joy.
    And now they never meet in grove or green,
    By fountain° clear or spangled starlight sheen,°
    But they do square,° that all their elves for fear   30
    Creep into acorn cups and hide them there.

FAIRY   Either I mistake your shape and making quite,
    Or else you are that shrewd° and knavish sprite

Stage Directions: The mood of aggressiveness and the building excitement continue in the forest. Puck and the Fairy enter at opposite doors, suggesting that they represent opposing sides; or perhaps Puck jumps out, trying to frighten her. Their confrontation immediately conveys the state of war in the forest.

1-15 Puck's "wander" (l. 1) implies that the Fairy does not know where she is going. The actor playing the Fairy should imagine what it takes to get through the briar and this will determine how she acts it out as she speaks. She wants to prove that she is the busiest, hardest-working fairy.

through (old form)

fenced land

(the moon was thought to move in a transparent sphere: each planet had its own)

fairy rings

bodyguards

marks of favor, gifts

fragrance

clown, lout

male fairies

exceedingly fierce and wrathful

(usually a child left by fairies in place of one they have stolen; here a stolen child)

travel through

by force

18-58 The Oberon and Titania conflict is set out before they come on. As Puck speaks, the Fairy gradually realizes just who he is and is awestruck. Finally she asks if he is who she thinks (ll. 32-34). Perhaps Puck looks at the audience as if to say, "That's me," and preens, making no attempt to stop her description. Puck is another version of Bottom: the narcissistic performer. He brags to the Fairy. His practical jokes are both funny and cruel; and they involve transformations.

spring;   gleam of light

confront each other, quarrel

mischievous

Called Robin Goodfellow. Are not you he
That frights the maidens of the villagery,   35
Skim milk° and sometimes labour in the quern,°
And bootless° make the breathless housewife churn,
And sometime make the drink to bear no barm,°
Mislead° night-wanderers, laughing at their harm?
Those that Hobgoblin call you and sweet Puck,   40
You do their work, and they shall have good luck.
Are not you he?

PUCK   Thou speakest aright;
I am that merry wanderer of the night.
I jest to Oberon and make him smile,
When I a fat and bean-fed° horse beguile,   45
Neighing in likeness of a filly foal;
And sometime lurk I in a gossip's° bowl,
In very likeness of a roasted crab,°
And when she drinks, against her lips I bob
And on her withered dewlap° pour the ale.   50
The wisest aunt, telling the saddest° tale,
Sometime for three-foot stool mistaketh me:
Then slip I from her bum, down topples she,
And "Tailor°" cries and falls into a cough;
And then the whole choir hold their hips and laugh,   55
And waxen° in their mirth, and neeze° and swear
A merrier hour was never wasted° there.
But room°, Fairy! Here comes Oberon.

FAIRY   And here my mistress. Would that he were gone!

Enter [OBERON], the King of Fairies, at one door,with his train;
and [TITANIA], the Oueen, at another with hers.

OBERON   Ill met by moonlight, proud Titania.   60

TITANIA   What, jealous Oberon? Fairies, skip hence.
I have forsworn his bed and company.

OBERON   Tarry, rash wanton.° Am not I thy lord?°

TITANIA   Then I must be thy lady. But I know
When thou hast stolen away from fairy land   65
And in the shape of Corin° sat all day,

i.e., steal the cream   hand-
   mill
to no effect
froth (on ale)
(with false fire; see III.i.93-7)

i.e., well fed

old woman's
crab-apple (used with sugar
   and spice to flavor hot ale)
fold of skin about neck (used
   of cattle)
most serious

(meaning unknown; perhaps
   referring to the "tail," or
   backside)
increase (old form)   sneeze
   (old form)
spent
make room

60-80 When Oberon enters he explodes in a fusil-
lade of consonants, as does Titania in her reply. It is
an angry confrontation that begins immediately as
they enter from opposite sides, with their armies. If
Oberon's fairies are male, Titania's female, the conflict is conveyed visually. The fairies are a physical,
psychological extension of Titania and Oberon,
which can be conveyed visually if when they move
their fairies move with them. Each group is a com-
hasty, self-indulgent creature   munity. There is a libidinous chaos in this scene, rep-
i.e., husband   resented by Oberon. At first, Titania speaks lightly,
teasing, aggravating him. But Oberon is in full flight of
madness, his emotions are out of control, he will not
(common names for shepherds   listen.
   in pastoral verse)

Playing on pipes of corn° and versing love
To amorous Philida.° Why art thou here,
Come from the farthest step° of India,
But that, forsooth, the bouncing° Amazon,   70
Your buskined° mistress and your warrior love,
To Theseus must be wedded, and you come
To give their bed joy and prosperity?

OBERON   How canst thou thus for shame, Titania,
          Glance at° my credit with Hippolyta,   75
          Knowing I know thy love to Theseus?
          Didst not thou lead him through the glimmering night
          From Perigenia, whom he ravishèd?
          And make him with fair Aegles break his faith,
          With Ariadne, and Antiopa?°   80

TITANIA   These are the forgeries of jealousy:
          And never, since the middle summer's spring,°
          Met we on hill, in dale, forest or mead,
          By pavèd° fountain or by rushy brook,
          Or in the beachèd margent° of the sea,   85
          To dance our ringlets° to° the whistling wind,
          But with thy brawls thou hast disturbed our sport.
          Therefore the winds, piping to us in vain,
          As in revenge, have sucked up from the sea
          Contagious° fogs; which falling in the land   90
          Hath every pelting° river made so proud
          That they have overborne their continents.°
          The ox hath therefore stretched his yoke in vain,
          The ploughman lost his sweat, and the green corn°
          Hath rotted ere his youth attained a beard;   95
          The fold stands empty in the drownèd field
          And crows are fatted with the murrion° flock;
          The nine men's morris° is filled up with mud,
          And the quaint° mazes in the wanton° green,°
          For lack of tread, are undistinguishable.   100
          The human mortals want° their winter here.
          No night is now with hymn or carol blessed;
          Therefore the moon, the governess of floods,
          Pale in her anger, washes° all the air
          That rheumatic° diseases do abound.   105

i.e., made of straw

(see line 66)

limit, reach

bragging, swaggering

in high hunting-boots

allude to

(all women loved and deserted by Theseus)

early midsummer

flowing over pebbles or stones

margin, shore

dances in a circular form   to the sound of

pestilential

paltry

banks

grain

i.e., dead from the "murrain," a fatal sheep disease

markings in turf for an outdoor game, like draughts

ingenious   quick-growing grass

lack

moistens

discharging rheum; i.e., colds, coughs, etc.

81-121 Titania begins her important speech in a feminine way by trying to reason with Oberon that their disagreement is insignificant compared with its consequences in the world at large. "On hill, in dale, forest or mead" (l. 83) echoes the Fairy at the beginning of the scene; such echoes build the world of the play: one of nature and the moon and night. Titania tries to make Oberon see that because of their conflict humanity is deprived of the proper change of seasons, which is the essence of the order of the universe.

"Human mortals" (l. 101) prompts the audience to feel sympathy for the suffering, shivering people. It is a reminder of the harsh weather of the real world. The universe is affected because they have contravened a governing moral order. As Titania describes the state of the world her fairies perhaps shed tears in sympathy. Oberon's fairies do not respond because he does not, except to resist doing so: he is hostile, defensive. Titania's two "our"s (l. 116) signal that she has shifted from accusing Oberon to taking full responsibility for her part in the feud. Her aim is to restore harmony. But he refuses to accept the mutual guilt she implies. Oberon abruptly changes his approach and tries to use his sexuality to get near Titania emotionally (ll. 119-21). Perhaps she stands still while he moves up to her, attempting to establish physical contact.

And thorough this distemperature° we see
The seasons alter: hoary-headed frosts
Fall in the fresh lap of the crimson rose,
And on old Hiems'° thin and icy crown
An odorous chaplet of sweet summer buds   110
Is, as in mockery, set. The spring, the summer,
The childing° autumn, angry winter change°
Their wonted° liveries; and the mazèd° world,
By their increase,° now knows not which is which.
And this same progeny of evils comes   115
From our debate,° from our dissension;
We are their parents and original.

OBERON   Do you amend it then; it lies in you.
Why should Titania cross her Oberon?
I do but beg a little changeling boy   120
To be my henchman.°

TITANIA   Set your heart at rest.
The fairy land buys not the child of me.
His mother was a vot'ress° of my order,
And in the spicèd Indian air by night,
Full often hath she gossiped by my side   125
And sat with me on Neptune's yellow sands,
Marking th'embarkèd traders° on the flood;
When we have laughed to see the sails conceive
And grow big-bellied with the wanton wind;
Which she, with pretty and with swimming gait   130
Following (her womb then rich with my young squire)
Would imitate, and sail upon the land
To fetch me trifles, and return again,
As from a voyage, rich with merchandise.
But she, being mortal, of that boy did die,   135
And for her sake do I rear up her boy:
And for her sake I will not part with him.

OBERON   How long within this wood intend you stay?

TITANIA   Perchance till after Theseus' wedding day.
If you will patiently dance in our round°   140
And see our moonlight revels, go with us.
If not, shun me; and I will spare° your haunts.

ill-humor/disturbance in
  nature, weather

the winter's

fruitful   exchange
accustomed   bewildered
(seasonal) produce

contention, quarrel

squire

122-45 Titania completes Oberon's verse line, suggesting that she does not pause before responding.
had taken the vows   Realizing Oberon will not change his mind about the
boy, she reveals what the child means to her. She
becomes vulnerable as she moves into her memory
and a female world. Dancing in a "round" (l. 140)
symbolizes concord, unity, order. Dance is a magical
i.e., merchant shipping   activity related to participation in the cosmic order.
Thus Oberon's refusal is significant. His abrupt
responses (ll. 138, 143) contrast with Titania's longer
explanations; he is not interested in how she feels;
he just wants the boy, wants to win. Finally she sees
that she cannot succeed by opening up to this man
because he is incapable of understanding, so she
goes back to the game, the contest. Titania is equal
to him; the difference is that she is in control, he is
not. He has not taken her seriously, and he has not
changed. Titania leaves Oberon standing there.
    This is a scene of pleading, not of attack: most-
ly Oberon is either moving away from Titania or
immobile. Her main job here in theatrical terms is to
evoke for him these scenes to prompt from him the
human responses of compassion and forgiveness.
This idea, possibility, goes to the philosophical heart
ring-dance   of the play. But even though this is a key statement
of philosophy, it occurs in a context that is as dra-
matic as anything in the play.
avoid

OBERON   Give me that boy, and I will go with thee.

TITANIA   Not for thy fairy kingdom. Fairies, away!
    We shall chide downright if I longer stay.   145
                        Exit [TITANIA *with her train.*]

OBERON   Well, go thy way. Thou shalt not from this grove
    Till I torment thee for this injury.°
    My gentle Puck, come hither. Thou rememb'rest
    Since° once I sat upon a promontory
    And heard a mermaid, on a dolphin's back,   150
    Uttering such dulcet and harmonious breath°
    That the rude° sea grew civil° at her song,
    And certain stars shot madly from their spheres°
    To hear the sea maid's music.

PUCK   I remember.

OBERON   That very time I saw (but thou couldst not)   155
    Flying between the cold moon and the earth,
    Cupid all armed. A certain° aim he took
    At a fair vestal° thronèd by° the west,
    And loosed his love-shaft smartly from his bow,
    As it should° pierce a hundred thousand hearts.   160
    But I might° see young Cupid's fiery shaft
    Quenched in the chaste beams of the wat'ry moon,
    And the imperial° vot'ress° passèd on,
    In maiden meditation, fancy-free.°
    Yet marked I where the bolt° of Cupid fell: 165
    It fell upon a little western flower,
    Before milk-white, now purple with love's wound;
    And maidens call it love-in-idleness.°
    Fetch me that flow'r, the herb I showed thee once.
    The juice of it, on sleeping eyelids laid,   170
    Will make or man or° woman madly dote
    Upon the next live creature that it sees.
    Fetch me this herb, and be thou here again
    Ere the leviathan° can swim a league.

PUCK   I'll put a girdle round about the earth   175
    In forty minutes   [*Exit.*]

OBERON   Having once this juice,
    I'll watch° Titania when she is asleep,

insult, affront

the time when

sound

turbulent   well-mannered

orbits

sure

virgin (probably an allusion to
   Queen Elizabeth I)   in

as if it would

could

majestic, queenly   i.e., she
   has vowed to serve Diana,
   goddess of chastity

free from thoughts of love

arrow

(the pansy, or hearts ease)

either... or...

sea-monster, whale

catch

146-87 In his selfish blindness, Oberon now wants revenge. Puck excitedly anticipates the chance to torture someone. The magical powers of Oberon, Puck, and the flower are introduced. And there is an explicit revelation of Oberon as male, bestial. His plan of revenge is akin to a rape, it is to be a degradation of Titania when she is most vulnerable. As in children's theatre, the audience is let in on his plans. The spectator is encouraged to identify with the evil, to share it. As in fairy tales, human limitations are transcended: invisibility, flight, and a magic flower are possible and one accepts in a desire to believe. Perhaps Oberon squats down with an eager Puck to give him his orders; it is an intimate, conspiratorial scene that the audience shares and they should be leaning forward to catch every word. In Brook's production, when Puck (John Kane) left he was raised on a trapeze. In the magic of the theatre, Oberon says he is invisible, so he is. As an onstage observer he is connected to the audience; he also demonstrates his desire to control events. Possibly he watches from an upper level, fascinated by what he sees and learns. Oberon (Ian Richardson) in Hall's 1962 production, had a habit of directly addressing the audience; he bowed mockingly on, "I am invisible" (Wardle).

And drop the liquor of it in her eyes.
The next thing then she waking looks upon
(Be it on lion, bear, or wolf, or bull,   180
On meddling monkey or on busy ape)
She shall pursue it with the soul° of love.
And ere I take this charm from off her sight
(As I can take it with another herb),
I'll make her render up her page to me.   185
But who comes here? I am invisible,
And I will overhear their conference.

Enter DEMETRIUS, HELENA *following him.*

DEMETRIUS   I love thee not; therefore pursue me not.
Where is Lysander and fair Hermia?
The one I'll slay, the other slayeth me.   190
Thou told'st me they were stol'n unto this wood;
And here am I, and wood° within this wood,
Because I cannot meet my Hermia.
Hence, get thee gone and follow me no more!

HELENA   You draw me, you hard-hearted adamant;°   195
But yet you draw not iron,° for my heart
Is true as steel. Leave you your power to draw,
And I shall have no power to follow you.

DEMETRIUS   Do I entice you? Do I speak° you fair?°
Or rather do I not in plainest truth   200
Tell you I do not, nor I cannot love you?

HELENA   And even for that do I love you the more.
I am your spaniel; and, Demetrius,
The more you beat me, I will fawn on you.
Use me but as your spaniel, spurn me, strike me,   205
Neglect me, lose me; only give me leave
(Unworthy as I am) to follow you.
What worser place can I beg in your love
(And yet a place of high respect with me)
Than to be usèd as you use your dog?   210

DEMETRIUS   Tempt not too much the hatred of my spirit,
For I am sick° when I do look on thee.

essence

and mad, frantic

mineral of great hardness/
lodestone, magnet
(of much less value than steel)

call, proclaim/speak with
beautiful/politely

188-213 Again harsh monosyllables, and negatives, begin another male-female confrontation, one to which the audience already knows the background. Demetrius has been searching for some time without finding Lysander and Hermia; he is frustrated, angry at Helena and grabs her (l. 189). The physical contact between the lovers is important. When he grabs her it is in anger, but Helena neither notices nor cares; she is in seventh heaven. Then he moves away from her (l.194), concerned with looking for Hermia and Lysander, and Helena moves to him (l. 195), only increasing his frustration, whereupon he moves back towards her, attacking again (l. 199).

Finally Demetrius collapses and Helena moves to him, trapping him, holding on to him; he is like a cornered animal, unable to escape, trying to shake her off.

nauseated

HELENA   And I am sick° when I look not on you.

DEMETRIUS   You do impeach° your modesty too much,
      To leave the city and commit yourself   215
      Into the hands of one that loves you not,
      To trust the opportunity of night
      And the ill counsel of a desert° place
      With the rich worth of your virginity.

HELENA   Your virtue° is my privilege.° For that   220
      It is not night when I do see your face,
      Therefore I think I am not in the night;
      Nor doth this wood lack worlds of company,
      For you, in my respect,° are all the world.
      Then how can it be said I am alone,   225
      When all the world is here to look on me?

DEMETRIUS   I'll run from thee and hide me in the brakes,°
      And leave thee to the mercy of wild beasts.

HELENA   The wildest hath not such a heart as you.
      Run when you will, the story shall be changed: 230
      Apollo flies and Daphne° holds° the chase;
      The dove pursues the griffin;° the mild hind°
      Makes speed to catch the tiger — bootless° speed,
      When cowardice pursues and valor flies.

DEMETRIUS   I will not stay° thy questions. Let me go!   235
      Or if thou follow me, do not believe
      But I shall do thee mischief in the wood.

HELENA   Ay; in the temple, in the town, the field,
      You do me mischief. Fie, Demetrius!
      Your wrongs do set a scandal on my sex.   240
      We cannot fight for love, as men may do;
      We should be wooed, and were not made to woo.
                                                        [*Exit* DEMETRIUS.]
      I'll follow thee and make a heaven of hell,
      To die upon° the hand I love so well.   [*Exit.*]

OBERON   Fare thee well, nymph.° Ere he do leave this grove,   245
      Thou shalt fly him, and he shall seek thy love.

faint, longing

discredit, call in question

deserted

merit, strength   authority

esteem, opinion

thickets

(the nymph who was pursed
    by the god Apollo and, at
    her own entreaty, changed
    into a laurel tree)   persists
    in

(fabulous beast, its upper part
    an eagle, the lower a lion)
    female deer

unavailing

wait for

by means of

semi-divine beings, imagined
    as maidens dwelling in
    woods

214-44 The threat of physical violence underlies the
scene; the madness and misunderstanding of the
play are very apparent. When unable to shake her off
he shifts to a different kind of threat, culminating in
the implication that she is in danger of being raped (ll.
214-19). There are fewer and fewer remnants of the
civilized world as the scenes in the wood progress.
This scene—she pleading, he bullying—leads one to
consider what kind of marriage they would have: an
unhappy mismatch.

Enter PUCK.

Hast thou the flower there?   Welcome, wanderer.

PUCK   Ay, there it is.

OBERON   I pray thee give it me.
　　I know a bank where the wild thyme blows,°
　　Where oxlips° and the nodding violet grows,   250
　　Quite overcanopied with luscious woodbine,°
　　With sweet musk-roses° and with eglantine:°
　　There sleeps Titania some time° of the night,
　　Lulled in these flowers with dances and delight,
　　And there the snake throws° her enamelled skin,   255
　　Weed° wide enough to wrap a fairy in.
　　And with the juice of this I'll streak her eyes
　　And make her full of hateful fantasies.
　　Take thou some of it and seek through this grove:
　　A sweet Athenian lady is in love   260
　　With a disdainful youth — anoint his eyes;
　　But do it when the next thing he espies
　　May be the lady. Thou shalt know the man
　　By the Athenian garments he hath on.
　　Effect it with some care that he may prove   265
　　More fond on° her than she upon her love:
　　And look thou meet me ere the first cock crow.

PUCK   Fear not my lord; your servant shall do so.   [*Exeunt.*]

Scene ii.   *Enter* TITANIA, *Queen of Fairies, with her train.*

TITANIA   Come, now a roundel° and a fairy song;
　　Then, for the third part of a minute, hence—
　　Some to kill cankers° in the musk-rose buds,
　　Some war with reremice° for their leathern wings
　　To make my small elves coats, and some keep back   5
　　The clamorous owl, that nightly hoots and wonders
　　At our quaint° spirits. Sing me now asleep.
　　Then to your offices,° and let me rest.

blooms

cross between cowslips and
    primroses

honeysuckle

sweet-smelling, rambling roses
    sweet briar

for some part of

casts off

garment

248-68 In Hall's production, when Puck (Ian Holm) returned after putting "a girdle round the earth," he popped up through the down-stage trap, "slightly puffed and dishevelled but triumphant" (Byrne, p. 555). In the Brook production, "Puck [swung] down on a trapeze, spinning a plate on a rod. Oberon, on a lower trapeze, look[ed] up to ask [if Puck had the flower] and Puck lean[ed] over to tip the still spinning plate on to Oberon's rod....The plate [did] not *become* the flower. Instead, the act of passing it [became] the *magic* of the flower" (Thomson, p. 126). As Oberon gives Puck his instructions Puck might almost pant with expectancy, like a dog waiting for a ball to be thrown. He is anxious to leave, but Oberon keeps clarifying and adding more instructions. Perhaps he knows how likely Puck is to make a mistake. Puck reassures Oberon, sensing his concern that his orders be followed correctly so peace will be restored.

infatuated with

round dance

canker-worms, caterpillars

bats

fine, dainty

duties

1-26 Titania returns, depressed and hurt. She must rest to restore her well-being, thus the dance and the song. Titania and her fairies convey the idea of loving care, the feminine world. Their song is about keeping evil away, and its soft sounds create a moment when the relentless, furious pace of the play stops.

On Brook's all-white stage Titania "float[ed] down from the flies in a crimson bower of ostrich feathers straight out of a Folies-Bergères review" (Roberts, p. 57); "for the lullaby...this was lowered to a mid-air position, and surrounded by four playground swings suspended at different levels but linked together, on which the four fairies sat in oriental squatting positions, arms raised with palms outwards to ward off danger" (Warren 1983, p. 55). Titania reassures her worried fairies; but the need for

Fairies sing.

1st Fairy	You spotted snakes with double° tongue,
	Thorny hedgehogs, be not seen; 10
	Newts and blindworms,° do no wrong,
	Come not near our Fairy Queen.

Chorus	Philomele,° with melody
	Sing in our sweet lullaby;
	Lulla lulla, lullaby, lulla, lulla, lullaby: 15
	Never harm
	Nor spell nor charm,
	Come our lovely lady nigh;
	So good night, with lullaby.

1st Fairy	Weaving spiders,° come not here; 20
	Hence, you long-legged spinners, hence!
	Beetles black, approach not near;
	Worm nor snail, do no offence.

Chorus	Philomele with melody, etc.

2nd Fairy	Hence, away! Now all is well. 25
	One aloof stand sentinel.

[Exeunt Fairies. Titania sleeps.]

Enter Oberon [and squeezes the flower on Titania's eyelids.]

Oberon	What thou seest when thou dost wake,
	Do it for thy true love take;
	Love and languish for his sake.
	Be it ounce,° or cat, or bear, 30
	Pard,° or boar with bristled hair,
	In thy eye that shall appear
	When thou wak'st, it is thy dear.
	Wake when some vile° thing is near. *[Exit.]*

Enter Lysander and Hermia.

Lysander	Fair love, you faint with wand'ring in the wood; 35
	And to speak troth°, I have forgot our way.
	We'll rest us, Hermia, if you think it good,
	And tarry for the comfort of the day.

forked

slow-worms (small, harmless
    snakes)

nightingale (raped and with
    her tongue cut out,
    Philomele in legend was
    metamorphosed into the
    bird)

(supposed to be poisonous)

a sentinel is a signal that she is aware of potential danger.

Where does Titania lie to sleep? On an Elizabethan stage like that at Stratford, Ontario, she can lie curled around one of the pillars supporting the balcony. She should not be in the way of the mechanicals or the lovers since the need to step over her would create unnecessary and distracting comic business. Perhaps the sentinel watches from above, and when Oberon comes on and sees the fairy he could zap her before she sees him; she would collapse, powerless, asleep.

In Hall's production, Puck, Oberon, and two full-sized attendants looked down on the tiny sentinel, unseen from above; "[a]t a signal from Oberon the kidnappers dropped lightly and in perfect unison to the ground, seized him, turned him upside down, presented him feet first to Oberon and Puck who hauled him up to the balcony in one quick movement, and carried him off into the forest"; he eventually returned to the scene—from the trap—"looking slightly the worse for wear" (Byrne, p. 556).

lynx
leopard

27-34 Oberon's words reveal his desire for cruel revenge: he wants Titania to be raped by a large animal. Immediately following the fairies' song, which banishes threatening animals, Oberon's speech is in harsh contrast. Ian Richardson, in the 1962 Hall production, "intone[d] his "spell" with "dyspeptic glee," emphasizing "vile" (Percival).

repulsive, (?) dangerous (cf.
    V.i.142,278)

truth

35-65 Another set of lovers who have been running through the woods enters noisily and upset: Lysander is lost and feels foolish. He runs on first, then Hermia enters, carrying her overnight bag, exhausted. Lysander is sincere when he suggests they should stop because Hermia looks tired, but he is also reluctant to admit he is lost; then he does

HERMIA   Be't so, Lysander. Find you out a bed;
    For I upon this bank will rest my head.   40

LYSANDER   One turf shall serve as pillow for us both,
    One heart, one bed, two bosoms, and one troth.

HERMIA   Nay, good Lysander. For my sake, my dear,
    Lie further off yet; do not lie so near.

LYSANDER   O take the sense, sweet, of my innocence!   45
    Love takes the meaning in love's conference.°
    I mean that my heart unto yours is knit,
    So that but one heart we can make of it:
    Two bosoms interchainèd with an oath—
    So then two bosoms and a single troth.   50
    Then by your side no bed-room me deny,
    For lying so, Hermia, I do not lie.

HERMIA   Lysander riddles very prettily.
    Now much beshrew° my manners and my pride,
    If Hermia meant to say Lysander lied.   55
    But, gentle friend, for love and courtesy
    Lie further off, in human modesty.
    Such separation (as may well be said)
    Becomes a virtuous bachelor and a maid.
    So far be distant; and good night, sweet friend: 60
    Thy love ne'er alter till thy sweet life end!

LYSANDER   Amen, amen, to that fair prayer say I;
    And then end life when I end loyalty!
    Here is my bed. Sleep give thee all his rest!

HERMIA   With half that wish the wisher's eyes be pressed!   65
                                        [*They sleep.*]

Enter PUCK.

PUCK   Through the forest have I gone,
    But Athenian found I none,
    On whose eyes I might approve°
    This flower's force in stirring love.
    Night and silence! Who is here?   70
    Weeds° of Athens he doth wear:
    This is he, my master said,

(l. 36). Rueful admission and a willingness to do what she wants inform his speech.

Civilized behavior and values reappear: love, courtesy, modesty, loyalty—the positive aspects of human relationships are recalled in the midst of this wood. As they settle in for the night Lysander is sexually aroused by the situation and the opportunity, but Hermia behaves according to the rules. The concern with where to lie is also important because when Puck comes in and makes his mistake the two are separated. When Brook's Hermia (Mary Rutherford) "decline[d] to sleep with Lysander, one of the fairies pull[ed] him back from her" (H. Dawson).

love interprets the talk of
lovers

curse (playful)

test

clothes

66-83 Puck comes on exhausted, very much as Hermia has; he cannot find the lovers to complete the task Oberon has set him. When he sees first Lysander (l. 70), then Hermia (l. 74), he moves between them. The juice on the eyes has its basis in children's theatre; it gives the audience the pleasure of being all-knowing, of participating in mischief with

Despisèd the Athenian maid;
And here the maiden, sleeping sound
On the dank and dirty ground.   75
Pretty soul, she durst not lie
Near this lack-love, this kill-courtesy.
Churl, upon thy eyes I throw
All the power this charm doth owe:°
When thou wak'st, let love forbid   80
Sleep his seat on thy eyelid.°

> [*He squeezes the juice on* LYSANDER'S *eyes.*]

So awake when I am gone,
For I must now to Oberon.   *Exit.*

Enter DEMETRIUS *and* HELENA, *running.*

HELENA   Stay, though thou kill me, sweet Demetrius.

DEMETRIUS   I charge thee, hence and do not haunt° me thus.   85

HELENA   O wilt thou darkling° leave me? Do not so.

DEMETRIUS   Stay, on thy peril! I alone will go.   [*Exit.*]

HELENA   O I am out of breath in this fond° chase!
    The more my prayer, the lesser is my grace.°
    Happy is Hermia, wheresoe'er she lies,   90
    For she hath blessèd and attractive eyes.
    How came her eyes so bright? Not with salt tears.
    If so, my eyes are oft'ner washed than hers.
    No, no! I am as ugly as a bear,
    For beasts that meet me run away for fear.   95
    Therefore no marvel though Demetrius
    Do, as° a monster, fly my presence thus.
    What wicked and dissembling glass of mine
    Made me compare° with Hermia's sphery eyne?°
    But who is here?   Lysander, on the ground!   100
    Dead, or asleep? I see no blood, no wound.
    Lysander, if you live, good sir awake!

LYSANDER [*Awaking.*]   And run through fire I will for thy sweet sake!
    Transparent° Helena! Nature shows art,°
    That through thy bosom makes me see thy heart.   105

possess

may he be so in love that he
  cannot sleep

follow

in the dark

infatuated, foolish
answer to prayer

as if I were

make comparisons   starry
  eyes

diaphanous, lightsome
  magic power

84-88 Another running entrance, and an explosion
of monosyllables alters the mood. But Helena adopts
a feminine approach: this is not how a man should
treat a woman. This is comic because this woman
has been behaving like an Amazon, has been the
aggressor; she suddenly implies that he should for-
get that and look at her as a weak woman.
Lysander's "I alone will go" (l. 87) conveys his frustration, his panic at being unable to shake her off. He
departs, and Hermia must decide whether to go after
him or not, but when she tries to she collapses.

In Hall's production, as soon as Helena
(Vanessa Redgrave) entered "she reache[d] towards
[Lysander (Albert Finney)], misse[d], and collapse[d]
on the floor; before long, she [was] screaming and
both [were] sitting on the floor, legs straight before
them, on the other side of the stage" (Brown 1960, p.
143). At one point during this scene in the Brook production, "Hermia, in a flying leap, hurl[ed] herself
across the middle of a door to prevent Lysander from
leaving as, in a marvel of split-second timing, he
reache[d] it in time to catch her" (Dukore, p. 93).

94-107 Helena is pitiful as she becomes aware she
has turned herself into a monster. As she paces she
comes on Lysander (l. 100). Possibly Helena asks
herself "who is here?" but she may address the audience, involving them. When Lysander awakes the
intensity of his language demonstrates immediately
and vividly how one tiny drop of Oberon's drug can
transform a person totally. There is nothing in
Lysander's experience to explain this moment; the
transformation is immediate and inexplicable in rational terms. In effect he is saying: "I will awake

Where is Demetrius? O how fit a word
Is that vile name to perish on my sword!

HELENA   Do not say so, Lysander, say not so.
What though he love your Hermia? Lord, what though?
Yet Hermia still loves you. Then be content.   110

DEMETRIUS   Content with Hermia? No! I do repent
The tedious minutes I with her have spent.
Not Hermia, but Helena I love:
Who will not change a raven for a dove?
The will° of man is by his reason swayed   115
And reason says you are the worthier maid.
Things growing are not ripe until their season:
So I, being young, till now ripe° not to reason.
And touching now the point° of human skill°,
Reason becomes the marshal to my will   120
And leads me to your eyes, where I o'erlook°
Love's stories written in love's richest book.

HELENA   Wherefore was I to this keen mockery born?
When at your hands did I deserve this scorn?°
Is't not enough, is't not enough young man,   125
That I did never— no, nor never can—
Deserve a sweet look from Demetrius' eye,
But you must flout° my insufficiency?
Good troth, you do me wrong— good sooth,° you do—
In such disdainful manner me to woo.   130
But fare you well. Perforce I must confess
I thought you lord of more true gentleness.°
O that a lady of° one man refused,
Should of° another therefore be abused!   *Exit.*

LYSANDER   She sees not Hermia. Hermia, sleep thou there,   135
And never mayst thou come Lysander near!
For, as a surfeit of the sweetest things
The deepest loathing to the stomach brings,
Or as the heresies that men do leave
Are hated most of° those they did deceive,   140
So thou, my surfeit and my heresy,
Of all be hated, but the most of° me!

because my life before this moment was sleep, I never thought you were this beautiful..." He thinks he sees correctly now, but the audience knows otherwise.

108-34 To Helena, Lysander is making a terrible mistake and she must bring him to his senses. At first she is friendly in her response, sorry for him. In Hall's 1959 production, at "who will not change a raven for a dove?" (l. 114), Lysander grabbed hold of Helena "and pull[ed] her around to face him, and soon Helena [was] lying on the stage with Lysander crouching close over her" (Brown 1960, pp. 143-44).

desire

Ironically, Lysander celebrates the moment of correct seeing by referring to reason to explain his love. Helena feels persecuted by all men. At first Lysander is overwhelmed, unmoving; but the sense of physical pursuit continues. Helena turns away, then turns back and begins to berate him. It is comic because, not only does he not see, he hardly hears: he is in a trance and continues to adore her despite what she says. The audience knows that because of the spell he is under, whatever she says he will not change, and this is funny. Helena flees, desperate; this is a nightmare for her and the audience should share her terror.

ripen, mature

highest point   reason, ability

peruse, read

taunt, insult

jeer at
very truly

good breeding, courtesy
by
by

135-44 Helena has not seen Hermia lying asleep, and Lysander pays no attention to her, does not really see her until Helena leaves. His language is excessive, in the best tradition of neo-platonic, pastoral poetry. He exits, chasing after Helena, just as Hermia awakens.

by

by

And, all my powers, address° your love and might
To honour Helen and to be her knight!   *Exit.*

HERMIA   [*Awaking*]   Help me, Lysander, help me! Do thy best   145
To pluck this crawling serpent from my breast!
Ay me, for pity!—What a dream was here!
Lysander, look how I do quake with fear.
Methought a serpent ate my heart away,
And you sat smiling at his cruel prey.°   150
Lysander!   What, removed? Lysander! Lord!
What, out of hearing? Gone? No sound, no word?
Alack, where are you? Speak, an if° you hear;
Speak, of all loves!° I swoon almost with fear.
No? Then I well perceive you are not nigh.   155
Either death or you I'll find immediately.   *Exit.*

prepare, direct

145-56 Hermia awakens thinking her dream is real and calls for help. At first the audience does not know why she wants to be helped, they just see a person waking up from a deep sleep, in extremis emotionally. Then she describes her dream, which for her is still real. Only then does she realize it was a dream. There is a gradual return to the real world from the world of dream, but the real world is worse than the dream world because she cannot escape it.

pillage, act of preying

Hermia gets up, walks in one direction then another looking for Lysander. Her questions are accompanied by physical action. It is dark and she is frightened. Her speech builds from her call—expecting an answer—to surprise, disbelief that he does not answer, to growing fear, to the point where she almost faints.

if

for love's sake

If Hermia and Lysander have brought luggage with them into the forest, when they run off here they leave it behind.

At this point in Brook's production Hermia fled from the fairies through the auditorium, as they sent the coils of wire they controlled "swirling out over the heads of the audience in sinister pursuit" (Warren 1983, p. 55).

ACT III

Scene i. *Enter the clowns:* [Q<small>UINCE</small>, S<small>NUG</small>, B<small>OTTOM</small>, F<small>LUTE</small>, S<small>NOUT</small>, *and* S<small>TARVELING</small>].

B<small>OTTOM</small>   Are we all met?

Q<small>UINCE</small>   Pat, pat;° and here's a marvellous convenient place for
our rehearsal. This green plot shall be our stage, this hawthorn
brake° our tiring-house;° and we will do it in action as we will
do it before the Duke.   5

B<small>OTTOM</small>   Peter Quince?

Q<small>UINCE</small>   What sayest thou, bully° Bottom?

B<small>OTTOM</small>   There are things in this comedy of Pyramus and Thisbe
that will never please. First, Pyramus must draw a sword to
kill himself; which the ladies cannot abide. How answer   10
you that?

S<small>NOUT</small>   By'r lakin,° a parlous fear.°

S<small>TARVELING</small>   I believe we must leave the killing out, when all is done.

B<small>OTTOM</small>   Not a whit. I have a device to make all well. Write me a
prologue, and let the prologue seem to say, we will do no   15
harm with our swords, and that Pyramus is not killed indeed;
and for the more better assurance, tell them that I Pyramus
am not Pyramus, but Bottom the weaver. This will put them
out of fear.

Q<small>UINCE</small>   Well, we will have such a prologue, and it shall be   20
written in eight and six.°

B<small>OTTOM</small>   No, make it two more; let it be written in eight and
eight.

S<small>NOUT</small>   Will not the ladies be afeared of the lion?

S<small>TARVELING</small>   I fear it, I promise you.   25

B<small>OTTOM</small>   Masters, you ought to consider with yourselves: to bring
in—God shield us!—a lion among ladies, is a most dreadful
thing. For there is not a more fearful wildfowl than your lion
living; and we ought to look to't.

Stage Directions: Perhaps Quince is the first to appear: he is early and has been waiting; he has had time to listen to the strange forest noises and become nervous, frightened. One of the other mechanicals might imitate the noise of an owl to add to Quince's fears. When the others enter, some might back in, looking around fearfully, bumping into things and jumping away, bumping into one another, then forming a little cluster for protection from the dangers they imagine. Only after they have gathered does Bottom arrive, taking over again. There is an echo of the first mechanicals' scene when Quince began with a similar question. What do they bring on with them? Lanterns perhaps. Do they bring work with them—such as sewing for the tailor? They will have their scripts and perhaps food. This is their only rehearsal and they are both enthusiastic and anxious.

apt, ready at the right time

thicket   dressing-room

good fellow, mate

1-19 Quince explains what they are to imagine: the stage where they will be performing at court. He has never seen his play performed and is eager to see it now, "in action" (l. 5). But Bottom is not ready to rehearse; he has read the script and sees problems: the first is Pyramus killing himself. For every problem Bottom raises he has a solution; it is like a game for him: "We need a balloon, we haven't got one, but I've got a paper in my pocket and will draw a picture of a balloon on it." His solutions are the essence of what theatre is: just a play and not to be taken literally.

by our lady (trivial oath)
  something to be terribly
  afraid of

20-39 Quince tries to take control but Bottom continues raising problems, so that a comic rhythm is created. Conscious of the need for speed, Quince agrees to Bottom's suggestions just to get on with it. Quince might walk around distractedly, establishing where the various locations are, not giving all his attention to Bottom.

    As before, Snout takes up Bottom's suggestions—a character is being developed, a nervous Nellie who cannot comprehend that this is all pretend. Snout represents the unsophisticated who cannot differentiate between art and life. Art is sophisticated because it involves representation, pretending, imagination. Snout starts thinking of solutions too; he is learning, but Bottom is always ahead of him with solutions that convey the excitement of a person of the theatre. When Snug learns he will have to speak, not just roar, he starts to think about going home.

verse-lines of eight and six syl-
  lables, alternately (a ballad
  meter)

SNOUT   Therefore another prologue must tell he is not a lion.   30

BOTTOM   Nay, you must name his name, and half his face must be
    seen through the lion's neck, and he himself must speak
    through, saying thus, or to the same defect: "Ladies," or
    "Fair ladies, I would wish you"—or "I would request you",
    or "I would entreat you—not to fear, not to tremble: my life   35
    for yours. If you think I come hither as a lion, it were pity of
    my life.° No! I am no such thing: I am a man, as other men
    are." And there indeed let him name his name, and tell
    them plainly, he is Snug the joiner.

QUINCE   Well, it shall be so. But there is two hard things: that   40
    is, to bring the moonlight into a chamber; for you know,
    Pyramus and Thisbe meet by moonlight.

SNOUT   Doth the moon shine that night we play our play?

BOTTOM   A calendar, a calendar! Look in the almanac; find out
    moonshine, find out moonshine.   45

QUINCE   Yes! It doth shine that night.

BOTTOM   Why, then may you leave a casement of the great
    chamber window, where we play, open; and the moon may
    shine in at the casement.

QUINCE   Ay; or else one must come in with a bush of thorns°   50
    and a lantern, and say he comes to disfigure,° or to present,°
    the person of Moonshine. Then there is another thing: we
    must have a wall in the great chamber; for Pyramus and
    Thisbe, says the story, did talk through the chink of a wall.

SNOUT   You can never bring in a wall. What say you, Bottom?   55

BOTTOM   Some man or other must present Wall: and let him have
    some plaster, or some loam or some roughcast,° about him,
    to signify Wall; and let him hold his fingers thus, and through
    that cranny shall Pyramus and Thisbe whisper.

QUINCE   If that may be, then all is well. Come, sit down every   60
    mother's son, and rehearse your parts. Pyramus, you begin.
    When you have spoken your speech, enter into that brake;
    and so every one according to his cue.

a bad thing for me

traditional accoutrement of the man in the moon; a bundle of sticks, sign that he was banished there for gathering them on the sabbath (?)

(for "figure, represent").....perform, personate

40-63 Quince challenges Bottom to find a solution and Bottom is stumped; again it is Snout who comes up with an answer: the real moon. But Bottom regains control, asking for a calendar. The others just stand there, looking at each other, dismayed, dumbfounded, but Quince has a calendar - perhaps in a big carpet-bag. All crowd so close around Quince that he is unable even to open the almanac and must break away from them. Quince finds the answer but cannot see how it helps; Bottom keeps them in suspense, waiting for the solution. They have dealt with the moon but now there is the wall, which seems an insurmountable problem to Snout; a really good actor will conjure up images of the Great Wall of China. This has not been thought through by Quince; it works in his imagination. But Bottom is in his element: he loves difficulties, loves rising to the occasion, and his solutions always require an audience to appreciate them.

mixture of lime and gravel

Enter ROBIN [PUCK].

PUCK   What hempen homespuns° have we swagg'ring here,
          So near the cradle° of the Fairy Queen?   65
          What, a play toward!° I'll be an auditor;
          An actor too perhaps, if I see cause.

QUINCE   Speak, Pyramus. Thisbe, stand forth.

PYRAMUS [BOTTOM]   Thisbe, the flowers of odious savors sweet—

QUINCE   Odors— "odorous!"   70

PYRAMUS   —odorous savors sweet;. . .
          So hath thy breath, my dearest Thisbe dear.
          But hark, a voice! Stay thou but here a while,
          And by and by° I will to thee appear.   *Exit.*

PUCK   A stranger Pyramus than e'er played here!   [*Exit.*]   75

THISBE [FLUTE]   Must I speak now?

QUINCE   Ay, marry, must you. For you must understand he goes
          but to see a noise that he heard, and is to come again.

THISBE   Most radiant Pyramus, most lily-white of hue,
          Of color like the red rose on triumphant brier,   80
          Most brisky Juvenal,° and eke° most lovely Jew,°
          As true as truest horse that yet would never tire,
          I'll meet thee, Pyramus, at Ninny's° tomb.

QUINCE   "Ninus' tomb," man. Why, you must not speak that
          yet. That you answer to Pyramus. You speak all your part°   85
          at once, cues and all. Pyramus enter. Your cue is past; it is
          "never tire."

THISBE   O! — as true as truest horse, that yet would never tire.

          [*Re-enter* PUCK, *and* BOTTOM *with an ass-head.*]

PYRAMUS   If I were fair,° Thisbe, I were only thine.

QUINCE   O monstrous! O strange! We are haunted. Pray,   90
          masters! Fly, masters! Help!
                              Exeunt all the clowns [*but* BOTTOM.]

crude rustics (dressed in
  homespun cloth of hemp)

i.e., her "bower" (see 1. 176,
  below)

in the making

64-67 During Puck's speech the mechanicals line
up to start the play. Perhaps Bottom comes on, does
not like his entrance, so goes and does it again; it is
an opportunity for a lot of stage business for Puck to
respond to. Puck might be on the balcony looking
down at them, separate but part of the scene. Or possibly he moves between them, reinforcing his invisibility for the audience. At line 65 comes a reminder of
Titania's presence after a long time of not being
aware of her. Puck sizes up the situation and sees an
irresistible opportunity for fun, a chance to be both
audience and participant.

70-89 The "odors—odorous" (l. 70) might signal
some action or reaction between the two words.
Perhaps Quince prompts Bottom with the right word,
and he resents the interruption but Quince persists.
There are also many opportunities for action by the
others. Flute's big moment is approaching; perhaps
confused about where he should be, he just stands
there at a loss, terrified and not really listening to
Bottom's dialogue.

soon

Quince becomes impatient but must explain
patiently to Flute (ll. 77-78). Flute just rattles off his
lines; clearly he has learned them, but just the words,
not the meaning. Quince begins to fear he has picked
the wrong guy. But Flute begins to catch on and
moves to where he is supposed to be, so Quince
goes back to his script. In Hall's production, during
the rehearsal Snug "wandered off and started sniffing
woodland flowers—only to be brought out of his
reverie by the accusing silence of the others"
(Addenbrooke, p. 116).

lively juvenile (affected)
  also (archaism)   (abbrevia-
  tion of Juvenal, or desperate
  rhyme for hue)

(ninny = fool)

script given to actor with his
  lines and cues for them

(Bottom's misreading; the
  comma should be after
  were)

PUCK   I'll follow you, I'll lead you about a round,°
    Through bog, through bush, through brake, through briar.
    Sometime a horse I'll be, sometime a hound,
    A hog, a headless bear, sometime a fire;°   95
    And neigh, and bark, and grunt, and roar, and burn,
    Like horse, hound, hog, bear, fire, at every turn.   *Exit.*

BOTTOM   Why do they run away? This is a knavery of them to
    make me afeard.

Enter SNOUT.

SNOUT   O Bottom, thou art changed! What do I see on thee?   100

BOTTOM   What do you see? You see an ass head of your own,
    do you?   [*Exit* SNOUT.]

Enter QUINCE.

QUINCE   Bless thee, Bottom, bless thee! Thou art translated.°

                                                       Exit.

BOTTOM   I see their knavery. This is to make an ass of me, to
    fright me if they could. But I will not stir from this place,   105
    do what they can. I will walk up and down here, and I will
    sing, that they shall hear I am not afraid.

[*Sings.*]   The ousel° cock so black of hue,
                With orange-tawny bill,
             The throstle° with his note so true,   110
                The wren with little quill°—

TITANIA [*Awaking.*] What angel wakes me from my flow'ry bed?

BOTTOM [*Sings.*] The finch, the sparrow, and the lark,
                The plain-song° cuckoo gray,
             Whose note full many a man doth mark   115
                And dares not answer nay—

    for, indeed, who would set his wit to° so foolish a bird? Who
    would give a bird the lie, though he cry "cuckoo°" never so?

TITANIA   I pray thee, gentle mortal, sing again.
    Mine ear is much enamored of thy note;   120
    So is mine eye enthrallèd to thy shape;

roundabout

will o'the wisp

90-97 When Bottom comes on with the ass's head, Puck the showman precedes him, eagerly awaiting the reaction of the others. Note that it is Puck who picks the ass; obeying Oberon's general orders to choose a beast, he makes it the one that will be the most fun for him. In both Hall's productions Bottom did not wear the traditional ass's head; instead the transformation was conveyed by hooves and flapping ears (Trewin, p. 515); in Brook's, Bottom wore "a button nose, ear muffs and clogs" (Styan, p. 228).

There is much opportunity for reaction from the frightened mechanicals, as Quince's fearful cries suggest. He immediately believes: all the tales of the forest he has heard are confirmed—here is a monster. There is a progression from Quince's "O monstrous" to "O strange" to "We are haunted" (l. 90); the one leads to the other, to the conclusion. At "Pray masters" (l. 91), perhaps he makes the sign of the cross as if to exorcise the evil. The others are unable to move, even Bottom, who cannot understand what Quince is talking about. Puck, meanwhile, doubles over in silent laughter. The frightened mechanicals flee in different directions, bumping into things, dropping lanterns, scripts, bags, and Puck follows to continue the fun by adopting animal disguises.

transformed

98-111 Mystified, Bottom comes up with an explanation: he sees it as a plot against him. Running in circles, Snout reenters, unable to believe his eyes. And Quince tiptoes back, perhaps to retrieve his bag, fearful but unable to leave it. He says "bless thee" (l. 103) to avoid awakening the monster's wrath. In his turn, Bottom attempts to understand what has happened. Bottom refuses to flee, because they are not going to make a fool of him. And he sings to seem brave; the irony is that his singing betrays his terror, as does his walking up and down, watching, looking about him.

blackbird

thrush
voice, song (lit. pipe)

with simple, repetitive song

against, to answer
cuckold

112-42 Titania's awakening echoes Lysander's when he awoke to a new vision of Helena. And unlike Quince, who saw a monster, Titania sees an angel. When does Bottom realize that she is speaking to him? Perhaps when she says "gentle mortal" (119) he looks behind him to see if she is talking to someone else. His realization that this beautiful Fairy

And thy fair virtue's force° perforce doth move me
On the first view to say, to swear, I love thee.

BOTTOM   Methinks, mistress, you should have little reason for
that. And yet, to say the truth, reason and love keep little   125
company together nowadays; the more the pity that some
honest neighbors will not make them friends. Nay, I can gleek°
upon occasion.

TITANIA   Thou art as wise as thou art beautiful.

BOTTOM   Not so, neither; but if I had wit enough to gèt out of   130
this wood, I have enough to serve mine own turn.

TITANIA   Out of this wood do not desire to go.
Thou shalt remain here, whether thou wilt or no.
I am a spirit of no common rate:°
The summer still° doth tend upon my state,°   135
And I do love thee; therefore go with me.
I'll give thee fairies to attend on thee,
And they shall fetch thee jewels from the deep,°
And sing while thou on pressèd flowers dost sleep;
And I will purge thy mortal grossness so,   140
That thou shalt like an airy spirit go.
Peaseblossom, Cobweb, Moth, and Mustardseed!

Enter four FAIRIES [*:*PEASEBLOSSOM, COBWEB, MOTH, *and* MUSTARDSEED].

PEASEBLOSSOM   Ready.

COBWEB   And I.

MOTH   And I.

MUSTARDSEED   And I.

ALL   Where shall we go?

TITANIA   Be kind and courteous to this gentleman:
Hop in his walks and gambol in his eyes;   145
Feed him with apricocks° and dewberries,°
With purple grapes, green figs and mulberries;
The honey bags steal from the humblebees,°
And for night tapers crop their waxen thighs
And light them at the fiery glowworm's eyes,   150

the power of your pure, moral excellence

make a joke

worth
always   greatness

i.e., pearls and corals

apricots (old form)   blackberries
bumblebees

Queen addresses him is a gradual process and invites a whole series of responses from the actor. When, embarrassed, Bottom makes a joke and laughs, at "friends" (l. 127), perhaps his laugh is a donkey's bray. Then Titania does to Bottom what Oberon has done to the sentinel, she charms him so he is unable to leave; she is in control.

143-58   To Titania's fairies, Bottom is the man in the moon who fell to earth, or Gulliver; their wonder and reverence are apparent in how they treat him. Bottom may have been turned into an ass, but to the fairies he is a gentleman: yet another transformation for him to cope with. He readily accommodates himself to this new role as a gentleman—and why not? As the fairies examine Bottom, he studies them, as full of wonder as they are. Titania wants to please Bottom, to stimulate his appetite. Her speech is not just a beautiful lyric moment, but sensuous, erotic: her intentions are sexual. The audience, who have seen Oberon put the juice on her eyes, are aware of why she sees and speaks as she does.

To have my love to bed and to arise;
And pluck the wings from painted butterflies
To fan the moonbeams from his sleeping eyes.
Nod to him, elves, and do him courtesies.

PEASEBLOSSOM   Hail, mortal!   155

COBWEB   Hail!

MOTH   Hail!

MUSTARDSEED   Hail!

BOTTOM   I cry your worships mercy,° heartily. I beseech your
worship's name.   160

COBWEB   Cobweb.

BOTTOM   I shall desire you of more acquaintance, good Master
Cobweb: if I cut my finger, I shall make bold with you.° Your
name, honest gentleman?

PEASEBLOSSOM   Peaseblossom.   165

BOTTOM   I pray you, commend me to Mistress Squash,° your
mother, and to Master Peascod, your father. Good Master
Peaseblossom, I shall desire you of more acquaintance too.
Your name I beseech you, sir?

MUSTARDSEED   Mustardseed.   170

BOTTOM   Good Master Mustardseed, I know your patience° well.
That same cowardly, giantlike ox-beef hath devoured many
a gentleman of your house. I promise you your kindred hath
made my eyes water° ere now. I desire you of more acquaintance, good Master Mustardseed.   175

TITANIA   Come wait° upon him; lead him to my bower.
            The moon methinks looks with a wat'ry eye;
            And when she weeps, weeps every little flower,
                Lamenting some enforcèd° chastity.
            Tie up my lover's tongue, bring him silently.   180
                            Exit [TITANIA *with* BOTTOM *and* FAIRIES.]

beg pardon of your honors
(for asking their names)

(cobwebs were used to stop
bleeding)

unripe pea pod (or *peascod*)

indulgence, sufferance (while
being *devoured* with the
beef)

i.e., with sympathy/because of
the sharp taste

attend

violated

159-72 As Titania watches Bottom admiringly, he begins to warm to his new role, to joke and enjoy himself. The fairies' names evoke folklore; it is a fairy-tale come to life for Bottom: not a world of princes and princesses but ordinary fairies, servants like he is. And he realizes that the things he has always seen, like a mustardseed or peaseblossom, are alive; his sense of them is transformed. He sees a new reality, another dimension in nature: its anthropomorphic quality.

But Titania just wants to get him into bed, and that must not be forgotten through this scene. In Brook's production as Titania fell in love with Bottom "she lay on her back and curled her legs around his, clawing at his thighs, gasping and gabbling in sexual frenzy... whereupon Bottom jumped on top of her" (Warren 1983, pp. 57-58).

173-77 At Titania's command perhaps the fairies all join hands to lead Bottom into the bower, and he is at the end of this chain. On "bower" (176) Titania looks at the moon, disturbed. There is the sense that the moon, Diana, knows what is being done to Titania, her creature, and is crying in sympathy. But the moon cannot counter the power of Oberon. For a moment Titania is shaken out of her enchantment, her passion for Bottom, and is aware of a disturbing element. The fairies and Bottom all stop and look up at the moon. At "chastity" (179) Bottom brays again so she tells her fairies to silence him, and we are back to the immediate moment.

In the Brook production the "climax" of the first part came here. "Titania's body arche[d] with desire, she crie[d] out, the fairies carrie[d] Bottom in state to her bed, an arm raised through his legs like a giant phallus, with Mendelssohn's 'Wedding March' bursting triumphantly on the audience and huge confetti paper plates showering down from the gallery" (Addenbrooke, p. 168).

Scene ii.   *Enter* [OBERON,]*King of Fairies, and* ROBIN
GOODFELLOW [PUCK].

OBERON   I wonder if Titania be awaked;
    Then what it was that next came in her eye,
    Which she must dote on in extremity.
    Here comes my messenger. How now, mad spirit!
    What night-rule° now about this haunted grove?   5

PUCK   My mistress with a monster is in love.
    Near to her close° and consecrated bower,
    While she was in her dull and sleeping hour,
    A crew of patches,° rude mechanicals,°
    That work for bread upon Athenian stalls,°   10
    Were met together to rehearse a play,
    Intended for great Theseus' nuptial day.
    The shallowest thickskin° of that barren sort,°
    Who Pyramus presented° in their sport,°
    Forsook his scene and entered in a brake.   15
    When I did him at this advantage take,
    An ass's nole° I fixèd on his head.
    Anon his Thisbe must be answerèd,
    And forth my mimic° comes. When they him spy,
    As wild geese that the creeping fowler eye,   20
    Or russet-pated choughs,° many in sort,°
    Rising and cawing at the gun's report,
    Sever themselves° and madly sweep the sky;
    So, at his sight, away his fellows fly
    And at our° stamp here o'er and o'er one falls;   25
    He murder cries, and help from Athens calls.
    Their sense thus weak, lost with their fears thus strong,
    Made senseless things begin to do them wrong,
    For briars and thorns at their apparel snatch:
    Some sleeves, some hats; from yielders° all things catch.   30
    I led them on in this distracted fear
    And left sweet Pyramus translated° there:
    When in that moment (so it came to pass)
    Titania waked, and straightway loved an ass.

disorder, revels of night-
time(?)

secluded, secret

fools, clowns   rough labor-
ing-men
shops, work-places

blockhead   useless lot, crew
acted   entertainment, play

1-40 Oberon awaits Puck's report impatiently, in a heightened state of expectation. For a director of the play Puck's description gives stage directions for the earlier action. Puck takes pleasure in telling Oberon what he has done; for the audience there is another kind of pleasure in knowing more than either Puck or Oberon. Trying to please Oberon, Puck concentrates on what he has done to Titania, and especially to the mechanicals; the lovers only come into it at the end, when Oberon asks (ll. 36-37). The audience gets a different perspective here: the lovers were frightened, but for Puck it was fun. As he speaks, Puck acts out what has happened and Oberon, his audience, is entertained, satisfied. Puck's language conveys the chaos he has created, and how he has enjoyed deceiving people's senses.

noddle, head

imitator, buffoon

grey-headed jackdaws   in a
large flock

scatter

our (royal plural; jocular)

i.e., those running away

transformed

OBERON   This falls out better than I could devise.   35
    But hast thou yet latched° the Athenian's eyes
    With the love juice, as I did bid thee do?

PUCK   I took him sleeping (that is finished too)
    And the Athenian woman by his side,
    That,° when he waked, of force she must be eyed.   40

Enter DEMETRIUS *and* HERMIA.

OBERON   Stand close.° This is the same Athenian.

PUCK   This is the woman, but not this the man.

DEMETRIUS   O why rebuke you him that loves you so?
    Lay breath so bitter on your bitter foe.

HERMIA   Now I but chide; but I should use thee worse,   45
    For thou, I fear, hast given me cause to curse.
    If thou hast slain Lysander in his sleep,
    Being o'er shoes° in blood, plunge in the deep
    And kill me too.
    The sun was not so true unto the day   50
    As he to me. Would he have stolen away
    From sleeping Hermia? I'll believe as soon
    This whole° earth may be bored, and that the moon
    May through the center creep, and so displease
    Her brother's° noontide with th' Antipodes.°   55
    It cannot be but thou hast murd'red him.
    So should a murderer look — so dead,° so grim.

DEMETRIUS   So should the murdered look; and so should I,
    Pierced through the heart with your stern cruelty.
    Yet you, the murderer, look as bright, as clear,   60
    As yonder Venus° in her glimmering sphere.°

HERMIA   What's this to° my Lysander? Where is he?
    Ah, good Demetrius, wilt thou give him me?

DEMETRIUS   I had rather give his carcass to my hounds.

HERMIA   Out, dog! Out, cur! Thou driv'st me past the bounds   65
    Of maiden's patience. Hast thou slain him then?
    Henceforth be never numb'red among men.

caught/(?) moistened

so that

41-44 When the lovers enter Puck learns he has made a mistake; he is deflated. Since Puck and Oberon must be on stage to observe the lovers, but not in the foreground, perhaps they watch what follows from the balcony. Oberon is furious at Puck's mistake and the tension between them continues through the scene. The dialogue of the two lovers begins *in medias res*, keeping the pace of the play hurtling forward.

concealed

so deep

45-87 Hermia's speech is hyperbolic: the only explanation she can think of for Lysander's disappearance is that Demetrius killed him out of jealousy, but she wants him to deny it. In her imagination Hermia has transformed Demetrius into a murderer, a beast. She cannot be dissuaded and responds not to Demetrius' words of love but to what she imagines; they talk at cross-purposes. For the audience, who know what has really happened, the misunderstanding is comic. Demetrius has no sooner escaped Helena than he is attacked by Hermia. Hermia pursues Demetrius around the stage, accusing him, then storms off. Demetrius collapses, the exhausted lover.

entire

i.e., the sun's   i.e., on the
   other side of the earth

deathly, deadly pale

evening star/goddess of love
   orbit

to do with

O once° tell true! Tell true, even for my sake!
Durst thou have looked upon him, being awake?
And hast thou killed him sleeping? O brave touch°!   70
Could not a worm,° an adder, do so much?
An adder did it; for with doubler° tongue
Than thine (thou serpent!) never adder stung.

DEMETRIUS   You spend your passion on a misprised° mood:°
I am not guilty of Lysander's blood,   75
Nor is he dead, for aught that I can tell.

HERMIA   I pray thee, tell me then that he is well.

DEMETRIUS   An if° I could, what should I get therefore?°

HERMIA   A privilege never to see me more.
And from thy hated presence part I so.   80
See me no more, whether he be dead or no.   *Exit.*

DEMETRIUS   There is no following her in this fierce vein.
Here therefore for a while I will remain.
So sorrow's heaviness° doth heavier° grow
For° debt that bankrupt sleep doth sorrow owe;   85
Which now in some slight measure it will pay,
If for his° tender° here I make some stay.   *Lies down [and sleeps.]*
OBERON   What hast thou done? Thou hast mistaken quite,
And laid the love juice on some truelove's sight.
Of thy misprision° must perforce ensue   90
Some true love turned, and not a false turned true.°

PUCK   Then fate o'errules that,° one man holding troth,°
A million fail, confounding° oath on° oath.

OBERON   About the wood go swifter than the wind,
And Helena of Athens look° thou find.   95
All fancy-sick° she is, and pale of cheer°
With sighs of love that costs the fresh blood dear.°
By some illusion see thou bring her here:
I'll charm his eyes against° she do appear.

PUCK   I go, I go; look how I go,   100
Swifter than arrow from the Tartar's bow.°   *[Exit.]*

OBERON   Flower of this purple dye,
            Hit with Cupid's archery,

for once

fine stroke (ironical)
snake
more forked/more deceitful

mistaken   anger/state of
    mind

Even if   for that

weariness,   more sorrowful,
    burdensome
because of

i.e., sleep's   offer

mistake
true love repulsed/changed

so that   faith
breaking   after

be sure to
love-sick   face, look
(each sigh was thought to
    expend a drop of blood)
ready for when

(Tartars were famed as violent
    and skilled warriors)

88-112 In his anger, Oberon perhaps twists Puck's ear, or kicks him. Puck is sent to fix the problem immediately. The phrasing of "I go, I go; look how I go" (l. 100) suggests that Puck pauses, perhaps for praise and attention: Oberon has dismissed him and angrily turned away but Puck cannot leave it at that. At "Swifter than arrow from the Tartar's bow" (l. 101) Oberon might finally look. Brook's Puck delivered these lines from the gallery as he sent a silver dish spinning from the top of his wand to that of Oberon ten feet below, both on trapezes (Fiddick).

Sink in apple° of his eye.
When his love he doth espy,   105
Let her shine as gloriously
As the Venus of the sky.
When thou wak'st, if she be by,
Beg of her for remedy.

Enter PUCK.

PUCK   Captain of our fairy band,   110
            Helena is here at hand;
            And the youth, mistook by me,
            Pleading for a lover's fee.°
            Shall we their fond pageant° see?
            Lord, what fools these mortals be!   115

OBERON   Stand aside. The noise they make
            Will cause Demetrius to awake.

PUCK   Then will two at once woo one;
            That must needs be sport alone;°
            And those things do best please me   120
            That befall prepost'rously.

Enter LYSANDER *and* HELENA.

LYSANDER   Why should you think that I should woo in scorn?
            Scorn and derision never come in tears.
            Look when° I vow, I weep; and vows so born,
            In their nativity all truth appears.   125
            How can these things in me seem scorn to you,
            Bearing the badge of faith° to prove them true?

HELENA   You do advance° your cunning more and more.
            When truth kills truth, O devilish-holy fray!
            These vows are Hermia's: wlll you give her o'er? 130
                Weigh oath with oath, and you will nothing weigh.
            Your vows to her and me, put in two scales,
            Will even weigh; and both as light as tales.°

LYSANDER   I had no judgement when to her I swore.

HELENA   Nor none, in my mind, now you give her o'er.   135

pupil

recompense
foolish scene, spectacle

in itself/unequalled, unique

113-21...Puck's "Shall we their fond pageant see?" (l. 114) is a reminder that this is a play, that human life is a play and we are players who act in ignorance, but as such it should not be taken too seriously. The description also anticipates the mechanicals' Pyramus and Thisbe play. Puck's wonderment at "mortals'" folly is profound. Oberon tells Puck what will happen (ll. 116-17), and Puck perhaps addresses the audience; if so he invites agreement, complicity.

whenever

i.e., his tears

display, use

mere fictions, falsehoods

122-37 Upon entering with Helena, Lysander picks up where he left off wooing her. The verse acquires a sonnet-like rhyme scheme here, befitting the subject. But at line 136 there is no rhyme as Lysander states a bare, unpleasant fact, only to have Demetrius' waking words contradict what he has just said. For the audience this is comic, but for the characters it is terrifying.

In Hall's 1962 production a "delighted, flattered smile... flickered across [Helena's (Diana Rigg)] face at the first impassioned declarations from Lysander and Demetrius" (Warren 1983, p. 49).

This long and difficult section of the play must be well choreographed if it is to work. First there are two characters, then three, then four; it is like a quadrille, and should be a delight to watch. There is a chase, a fight, tricks; it can be very acrobatic. Do both men wear their swords through the forest scenes? What do they do with them, do they sleep with them on? Eventually they will have a sword fight, when they must be wearing them.

LYSANDER   Demetrius loves her, and he loves not you.

DEMETRIUS [*Awaking*.] O Helen, goddess, nymph, perfect, divine!
    To what, my love, shall I compare thine eyne°?·
    Crystal is muddy. O how ripe° in show
    Thy lips, those kissing cherries, tempting grow!   140
    That pure congealèd white, high Taurus° snow,
    Fanned with the eastern wind, turns to a crow
    When thou hold'st up thy hand: O let me kiss
    This princess° of pure white, this seal° of bliss!

HELENA   O spite! O hell! I see you all are bent   145
    To set against° me for your merriment.°
    If you were civil° and knew courtesy,
    You would not do me thus much injury.
    Can you not hate me, as I know you do,
    But you must join in souls to mock me too?   150
    If you were men, as men you are in show,
    You would not use a gentle° lady so;
    To vow, and swear, and superpraise my parts,°
    When I am sure you hate me with your hearts.
    You both are rivals, and love Hermia;   155
    And now both rivals to mock Helena.
    A trim° exploit, a manly enterprise,
    To conjure tears up in a poor maid's eyes
    With your derision! None of noble sort°
    Would so offend a virgin and extort°   160
    A poor soul's patience, all to make you sport.

LYSANDER   You are unkind, Demetrius. Be not so,
    For you love Hermia! This you know I know.
    And here with all good will, with all my heart,
    In Hermia's love I yield you up my part;   165
    And yours of Helena to me bequeath,°
    Whom I do love and will do till my death.

HELENA   Never did mockers waste more idle° breath.

DEMETRIUS Lysander, keep thy Hermia; I will none.°
    If e'er I loved her, all that love is gone.   170
    My heart to her but as guestwise sojourned,°
    And now to Helen is it home returned,
    There to remain.

eyes (archaic)
full and red

mountain range in Turkey

paragon   pledge, confirmation

make an attack upon   entetainment, amusement
well-mannered

mild/noble
character

fine (ironical)

rank
torture

assign, give over

useless, foolish

I want no part of her

travelled/lodged

138-68   Demetrius's hyperbole infuriates Helena and she explodes in a long tirade about how badly she has been treated. As Helena speaks the two men both try to get near her, touch her, but she shakes them off. When Demetrius moves close to her, Lysander intervenes and vice versa. They all have their own objectives here: each man feels he is the one who will get her; she is angry at both.

Helena has stopped trying to be the "dove;" the polite veneer is gone. At first she is outraged, feels she has been rejected, mocked. Then from line 155 there is the sense that she has figured it out (she is wrong, but does not know it); this confirms what she has long believed, that all are against her.

To Lysander she is accusing Demetrius and, seeing himself blameless, he turns on him (l. 162). This confrontation might be staged with Helena at the apex of a triangle, Lysander and Demetrius standing with their backs to the audience, watching her adoringly. To her they seem to be playing roles, deceiving her. After listening to them she makes a dismissive comment (l. 168), perhaps to the audience, the only possible source of sympathy.

169-76   Demetrius speaks first to Lysander, and when he mentions Helena turns to her, perhaps kneeling in front of her. Lysander might drag Demetrius away and kneel himself (l. 173), only to have Demetrius reverse the process again, giving a physical manifestation of the contest for Helena. They almost come to blows here as the tension between them builds. As Lysander looks at Helena, Demetrius sees Hermia coming. Perhaps Hermia has one shoe on and one shoe off; if so she would be even shorter when her stature is referred to later.

LYSANDER   Helen, it is not so.

DEMETRIUS   Disparage not the faith thou dost not know,
     Lest to thy peril thou aby° it dear:°   175
     Look where thy love comes; yonder is thy dear.

                            Enter HERMIA.

HERMIA   Dark night, that from the eye his function takes,
     The ear more quick of apprehension makes;
     Wherein it doth impair the seeing sense,
     It pays the hearing double recompense.   180
     Thou art not by mine eye, Lysander, found;
     Mine ear, I thank it, brought me to thy sound.
     But why unkindly didst thou leave me so?

LYSANDER   Why should he stay whom love doth press to go?

HERMIA   What love could press Lysander from my side?   185

LYSANDER   Lysander's love, that would not let him bide —
     Fair Helena: who more engilds the night
     Than all yon fiery oes and eyes° of light.
     Why seek'st thou me? Could not this make thee know,
     The hate I bare thee made me leave thee so?   190

HERMIA   You speak not as you think: it cannot be.

HELENA   Lo, she is one of this confederacy!
     Now I perceive they have conjoined all three
     To fashion this false sport in spite of me.°
     Injurious Hermia, most ungrateful maid,   195
     Have you conspired, have you with these contrived
     To bait° me with this foul derision?
     Is all the counsel that we two have shared,
     The sister's vows, the hours that we have spent,
     When we have chid the hasty-footed time   200
     For parting us — O is all forgot?
     All schooldays, friendship, childhood innocence?
     We, Hermia, like two artificial° gods,
     Have with our needles created both one flower,
     Both on one sampler, sitting on one cushion,   205
     Both warbling of one song, both in one key;°

atone, pay for   dearly

i.e., stars (*oes*= spangles, dress
ornaments; pun on letters
"o" and "i")

to spite me

harrass, torment

skillful, cunning

in mental accord (see *minds*,
207)

177-92   What do the two men do while Hermia
speaks? Perhaps Lysander just stands there loathing
her, while Demetrius takes the opportunity to get
nearer Helena. This must not be distracting because
Hermia's soliloquy-like speech about perception is
important thematically. When she finishes, the action
picks up again. This is the first time in the play the
four lovers are on stage together and their relationships at this point can be conveyed by how and
where they move. They become gradually more
acrobatic, active. At line 185 Hermia addresses
Lysander, he begins his answer to her, then turns to
Helena, then back to Hermia with his question and
statement of hate (l. 190). Hermia just turns away
from him, dismissing the possibility, it seems so
absurd to her. Helena's response is to laugh uncon-
trollably, perhaps looking at the audience, to include
them in the joke (l. 192).

192-97   Immobile, Helena takes it all in until she puts
the puzzle together, and it all fits when she sees that
Hermia is part of the conspiracy against her: "Now I
perceive" (l. 193). The "they" suggests that this too is
addressed to the audience. On the one hand this is a
moment of triumph for Helena, on the other the realization is terrible. The triumph, the sense of knowledge prevails: she can make sense of things and feel
relief even as she is horrified. Perhaps as she speaks
Demetrius, seeing Lysander occupied trying to shake
off Hermia, takes advantage of this and moves to
Helena; but each time he does so she fends him off,
he backs away, then tries to move close again. If
Helena has spoken the first two lines to the audience,
she then turns on Hermia, accusing her.

198-21   Helena tries to evoke in Hermia memories
of their friendship, to regenerate it. She reminds her
of all the feminine bonds they have, suggesting that
they should preclude Hermia's betrayal of her for the
men. Innocent, Hermia is mystified. Perhaps at line
198 Helena goes to Hermia, putting her arm around
her, and they sit down side by side. As she recalls
their idyllic female past she forgets the situation, and
Hermia of course agrees, finally even crying with the
joy of remembering their oneness. By line 208
Hermia might have her head on Helena's shoulder.
This completely excludes the two men. They stand
unmoving, enchanted by the beauty of the picture
evoked and adoring Helena, who is speaking.
        Then Helena accuses Hermia, in an abrupt shift
of tone (l. 215); if they are seated Helena would

As if our hands, our sides, voices, and minds,
Had been incorporate.° So we grew together,
Like to a double cherry, seeming parted,
But yet an union in partition,   210
Two lovely berries molded on one stem;
So with two seeming bodies, but one heart—
Two of the first,° like coats in heraldry,
Due but to one,° and crownèd with one crest.°
And will you rent° our ancient love asunder,   215
To join with men in scorning your poor friend?
It is not friendly, 'tis not maidenly.
Our sex, as well as I, may chide you for it,
Though I alone do feel the injury.

HERMIA   I am amazèd at your passionate words.   220
I scorn you not: it seems that you scorn me.

HELENA   Have you not set Lysander, as in scorn,
To follow me and praise my eyes and face?
And made your other love, Demetrius
(Who even but now did spurn me with his foot),   225
To call me goddess, nymph, divine and rare,
Precious, celestial? Wherefore speaks he this
To her he hates? And wherefore doth Lysander
Deny your love (so rich within his soul)
And tender me (forsooth) affection,   230
But by your setting on, by your consent?
What though I be not so in grace as you,
So hung upon with love, so fortunate;
But miserable most, to love unloved?
This you should pity rather than despise.   235

HERMIA   I understand not what you mean by this.

HELENA   Ay, do! Persever, counterfeit sad° looks,
Make mouths upon me when I turn my back,
Wink each at other, hold the sweet jest up.°
This sport, well carried, shall be chronicled.   240
If you have any pity, grace, or manners,
You would not make me such an argument.°
But fare ye well. 'Tis partly my own fault,
Which death or absence soon shall remedy.

combined, unified

two halves of one shield, of
the same color

granted to one person   sur-
mounted by a single crest (a
hart or heart)

tear

abruptly rise. She remembers how angry she is and
why. The two men react to the new tone and are
reminded of how they want Hermia out of the way.
Helena again introduces the idea of male against
female, trying to get Hermia to agree and leave with
her. Hermia cannot make sense of it since for her
nothing has changed (ll. 220-21). Helena interprets
Hermia's response as determination to keep up the
charade.

222-46   Helena begins to accuse Hermia and give
proofs for her conclusions, still trying to win Hermia to
her side. Hermia just stands there. The men watch
Helena, admiring her in her anger. Helena moves
back and forth depending on whom she accuses or
refers to, unable to keep still. The two men might be
in the same area upstage, Hermia alone downstage
and Helena moving between them. When Hermia
professes innocence (l. 236) Helena becomes angri-
er. Helena's accusations (ll. 237-39) suggest that the
two men have acted or reacted in a way that Helena
misinterprets. Her speech alternates between injury
and rage. At line 243 Helena starts to leave, she has
had enough; but perhaps she immediately realizes
she is in the forest and has nowhere safe to go.
Lysander moves to stop her, so does Demetrius.

serious

keep on with joke you enjoy
so much

subject (for your quarrel)

LYSANDER   Stay, gentle Helena; hear my excuse: 245
    My love, my life, my soul, fair Helena!

HELENA   O excellent!

HERMIA   Sweet, do not scorn her so.

DEMETRIUS   If she cannot entreat, I can compel.

LYSANDER   Thou canst compel no more than she entreat:
    Thy threats have no more strength than her weak prayers.   250
    Helen, I love thee; by my life, I do!
    I swear by that which I will lose for thee,
    To prove him false that says I love thee not.

DEMETRIUS   I say I love thee more than he can do.

LYSANDER   If thou say so, withdraw and prove it° too.   255

DEMETRIUS   Quick, come!

HERMIA   Lysander, whereto tends all this?

LYSANDER   Away, you Ethiope!°

DEMETRIUS   No, no; he'll
    Seem to break loose; take on° as he would follow,
    But yet come not. You are a tame man, go!

LYSANDER   Hang off, thou cat, thou burr! Vile thing, let loose,   260
    Or I will shake thee from me like a serpent!

HERMIA   Why are you grown so rude!° What change is this,
    Sweet love?

LYSANDER   Thy love! Out, tawny Tartar, out!
    Out, loathèd med'cine! O hated potion, hence!

HERMIA   Do you not jest?

HELENA   Yes, sooth; and so do you.   265

LYSANDER   Demetrius, I will keep my word with thee.

DEMETRIUS   I would I had your bond°, for I perceive
    A weak bond° holds you. I'll not trust your word.

LYSANDER   What, should I hurt her, strike her, kill her dead?
    Although I hate her, I'll not harm her so.   270

247-77   Thinking Lysander is mocking Helena, Hermia goes to her defense (l. 247). Lysander might pull Demetrius away from Helena; Demetrius draws his sword; perhaps Hermia goes to Lysander, clinging to him, and Demetrius interprets this as Lysander using Hermia as a shield. In fact Lysander cannot move; each time he manages to break loose Hermia grabs hold again. This continues for some time, with Demetrius possibly leaning against a tree, sword in hand, laughing at Lysander, mocking him (ll. 267-68). In complete frustration Lysander asks if he must kill Hermia to prove he does not love her. If she has been clinging to Lysander, Hermia lets go of him when he says he hates her (l. 270). It seems to her as if a transformation has occurred; she can find no explanation for it, but she realizes that this is not a dream; it is for real.

i.e., fight a duel to *prove* your love

(insultingly: Hermia is dark; see l. 263)

pretend

ungentle, brutal

written contract
restraint

HERMIA   What, can you do me greater harm than hate?
           Hate me! Wherefore? O me, what news, my love!
           Am not I Hermia? Are not you Lysander?
           I am as fair now as I was erewhile.
           Since night you loved me; yet since night you left me.   275
           Why then you left me — O the gods forbid! —
           In earnest, shall I say?

LYSANDER   Ay, by my life!
           And never did desire to see thee more.
           Therefore be out of hope, of question, of doubt;
           Be certain, nothing truer. 'Tis no jest   280
           That I do hate thee, and love Helena.

HERMIA   O me! You juggler,° you canker blossom,°
           You thief of love! What, have you come by night
           And stol'n my love's heart from him?

HELENA   Fine, i 'faith!
           Have you no modesty, no maiden shame,   285
           No touch of bashfulness? What, will you tear
           Impatient answers from my gentle tongue?
           Fie, fie, you counterfeit, you puppet, you!

HERMIA   Puppet? Why so? Ay, that way goes the game.
           Now I perceive that she hath made compare   290
           Between our statures; she hath urged her height,
           And with her personage, her tall personage,
           Her height (forsooth), she hath prevailed with him.
           And are you grown so high in his esteem,
           Because I am so dwarfish and so low?   295
           How low am I, thou painted maypole? Speak!
           How low am I? I am not yet so low
           But that my nails can reach unto thine eyes.

HELENA   I pray you, though you mock me, gentlemen,
           Let her not hurt me. I was never curst;°   300
           I have no gift at all in shrewishness;
           I am a right maid for my cowardice.
           Let her not strike me. You perhaps may think,
           Because she is something lower than myself,
           That I can match her.

277-88 When a relieved Lysander jumps in to affirm what he has said, Hermia turns on Helena. Through this section Hermia tries to get near Helena and tear her hair out. The change in Hermia is extreme and Lysander looks at her in surprise: she has seemed a vulnerable, hurt little girl needing protection; suddenly she turns into an Amazon, a virago. These women have that animus in them, which they carefully hide, but now it is visible. Helena and Hermia now focus on one another, wanting revenge for the betrayal, the conspiracy that each thinks the other has perpetrated on her. This major change affects the two men: they are surprised at the unexpected behaviour and move to defend Helena from Hermia.

When Hermia calls Helena a "canker blossom" (l. 282), she might try to get closer to her. When Helena suggests Hermia has "no modesty" (l. 285), she might move to her, but with some hesitation, some fear of what Hermia might do. Helena has seen Hermia on the warpath before and knows what a monster she can be when aroused. "Counterfeit" and "puppet" (l. 288) are like two gunshots, two challenges that Helena throws out; she strikes Hermia's achilles heel, and Hermia responds in kind, with the focus now on the physical. It becomes a very female fight.

trickster   canker-worm
(destroying flowers)

289-305 Hermia's "Ay, that way goes the game," and her new perceptions might be directed at the audience; both women look to the audience for sympathy, and each interprets events her own way. At the shift from "she" to "you" (l. 294), Hermia turns back to Helena. The men, holding the women apart, respond from moment to moment as the argument progresses. The insults become progressively more hurtful. At lines 296-98 Hermia moves to attack Helena physically; perhaps the two men grab her and pick her up so she is pedalling in the air, trying to get near Helena, who now is hiding behind Lysander. Brook's Hermia, "rant[ed] helplessly at Helena and the two men... struggle[d] to hold onto a trapeze that lift[ed] her into the air as she helplessly kick[ed] at them"(Dukore, p. 94).

shrewish, vicious

At "cowardice" (l. 302) Hermia breaks away from the two men, prompting Helena's "Let her not strike me" (l. 303). She is able to break away because the two men have been listening sympathetically to Helena's pleas. At Helena's cry, the men catch Hermia again, giving Helena the chance to hide behind the men as Hermia keeps maneuvering

HERMIA   Lower! Hark again!   305

HELENA   Good Hermia, do not be so bitter with me.
   I evermore did love you, Hermia,
   Did ever keep your counsels, never wronged you;
   Save that, in love unto Demetrius,
   I told him of your stealth° unto this wood.   310
   He followed you; for love I followed him.
   But he hath chid me hence, and threatened me
   To strike me, spurn me; nay, to kill me too.
   And now, so you will let me quiet go,
   To Athens will I bear my folly back   315
   And follow you no further. Let me go.
   You see how simple and how fond° I am.

HERMIA   Why, get you gone. Who is't that hinders you?

HELENA   A foolish heart, that I leave here behind.

HERMIA   What, with Lysander?

HELENA   With Demetrius.   320

LYSANDER   Be not afraid: she shall not harm thee, Helena.

DEMETRIUS   No sir, she shall not, though you take her part.

HELENA   O when she's angry, she is keen° and shrewd!°
   She was a vixen when she went to school;
   And though she be but little, she is fierce.   325

HERMIA "Little" again! Nothing but "low" and "little"!
   Why will you suffer her to flout me thus?
   Let me come to her.

LYSANDER   Get you gone, you dwarf!
   You minimus° of hind'ring knotgrass° made!
   You bead, you acorn!

DEMETRIUS   You are too officious   330
   In her behalf that scorns your services.
   Let her alone. Speak not of Helena;
   Take not her part. For if thou dost intend
   Never so little show of love to her,
   Thou shalt aby° it.

to get at her. Even if she thinks they are conspiring against her, she needs their protection. Lines 303-05 might be addressed to the audience as each tries to get their sympathy.

306-28   Finally Helena tries to explain, to inject a note of sanity, a way out of the confusion. At line 316 she gives up: "Let me go" she says, but no one is holding her; the men are holding Hermia, who asks Helena who is stopping her (l. 318). Helena begins to walk away, but swings around on Hermia's question, yelling in frustration, "A foolish heart..." (l. 319). In response Hermia breaks away and Lysander moves to protect Helena, prompting Demetrius to intervene; again the tension builds to a fight. Helena reveals another side of Hermia's nature (ll. 323-25), prompting Hermia to try to get at her again (l. 328).

stealing away

affectionate, doting, foolish

bitter, sharp   ill-natured

329-44 Now Lysander picks up on what Helena has said. His images become smaller and smaller, and more graphic. In two lines he reduces her to nothing, to something inanimate: "acorn" (l. 329). Demetrius interrupts; although he tells Lysander to let Hermia alone (l. 332), it seems that she is holding on to him and Lysander does something to free himself (l. 335). Hermia demonstrates her toughness: holding on to Lysander, biting, kicking, proving what Helena has said about her temper. When the men leave to fight it out, the women are left alone; there is no one to prevent Hermia from attacking Helena, who runs away in fear. Hermia wanders off, still mystified by what has happened.

most tiny creature   low-growing weed (supposed to stunt growth, used medicinally)

pay for

LYSANDER   Now she holds me not: 335
   Now follow, if thou dar'st, to try whose right,
   Of thine or mine, is most in Helena.

DEMETRIUS   Follow! Nay, I'll go with thee, cheek by jowl.
                 [*Exeunt* LYSANDER *and* DEMETRIUS.]
HERMIA   You, mistress, all this coil° is 'long of you.°
   Nay, go not back.

HELENA   I will not trust you, I,   340
   Nor longer stay in your curst company.
   Your hands than mine are quicker for a fray;
   My legs are longer though, to run away.

HERMIA   I am amazed, and know not what to say.
                 Exeunt [HELENA *and* HERMIA.]
OBERON   This is thy negligence. Still° thou mistak'st,   345
   Or else committ'st thy knaveries willfully.

PUCK   Believe me, King of Shadows,° I mistook.
   Did not you tell me I should know the man
   By the Athenian garments he had on?
   And so far blameless proves my enterprise,   350
   That I have 'nointed an Athenian's eyes;
   And so far am I glad it so did sort,°
   As this their jangling° I esteem a sport.

OBERON   Thou see'st these lovers seek a place to fight.
   Hie° therefore Robin, overcast the night.   355
   The starry welkin° cover thou anon
   With drooping fog as black as Acheron;°
   And lead these testy° rivals so astray,
   As° one come not within another's way.
   Like to Lysander sometime frame thy tongue,   360
   Then stir Demetrius up with bitter wrong;
   And sometime rail thou like Demetrius.
   And from each other look thou lead them thus,
   Till o'er their brows death-counterfeiting sleep
   With leaden legs and batty° wings doth creep.   365
   Then crush this herb into Lysander's eye,
   Whose liquor hath this virtuous° property,
   To take from thence all error with his° might,

turmoil   due to you

always, continually

darkness/spirits

turn out
wrangling

speed
sky (poetic)
river in Hades, the under-
    world
headstrong, aggressive
that

bat-like

efficacious
its

345-95 Oberon is angry, even suggesting that Puck
has confused things on purpose, and might strike at
Puck as he speaks. Certainly Puck has enjoyed the
confusion, but Oberon wants it resolved so he can
get back to his revenge on Titania; he tells Puck
exactly how to sort out the lovers. His aim now is
"peace" (l. 377) for all, perhaps suggesting that the
fighting between the four lovers has altered his feelings about Titania.

And make his eyeballs roll with wonted sight.
When they next wake, all this derision   370
Shall seem a dream and fruitless vision,
And back to Athens shall the lovers wend
With league, whose date° till death shall never end.
Whiles I in this affair do thee employ,
I'll to my queen and beg her Indian boy;   375
And then I will her charmèd° eye release
From monster's view, and all things shall be peace.

PUCK   My fairy lord, this must be done with haste,
For night's swift dragons°cut the clouds full fast,
And yonder shines Aurora's harbinger;°   380
At whose approach ghosts, wand'ring here and there,
Troop home to churchyards. Damnèd spirits° all,
That in crossways and floods have burial,
Already to their wormy beds are gone;
For fear lest day should look their shames upon,   385
They willfully themselves exile from light,
And must for aye consort° with black-browed night.

OBERON   But we are spirits of another sort.
I with the morning's love have oft made sport,°
And like a forester the groves may tread,   390
Even till the eastern gate, all fiery-red,
Opening on Neptune with fair blessèd beams,
Turns into yellow gold his salt green streams.
But notwithstanding, haste; make no delay:
We may effect this business yet ere day.   [*Exit.*]   395

PUCK   Up and down, up and down,
                   I will lead them up and down:
                   I am feared in field and town:
                   Goblin,° lead them up and down.
Here comes one.   400

Enter LYSANDER.

LYSANDER   Where art thou, proud Demetrius? Speak thou now.

PUCK   Here villain; drawn° and ready. Where art thou?

LYSANDER   I will be with thee straight.

duration

enchanted

(the chariot of Cynthia, moon
goddess, was drawn by
dragons across the sky)
dawn's herald, the morning
star
(Suicides were buried at cross-
roads, unless they drowned
themselves at sea; their
ghosts were thought to be
the first to disappear before
dawn)

keep company

i.e., Oberon has hunted with
Cephalus, Aurora's lover

i.e., Puck himself, or
Hobgoblin

with drawn sword

400-17 The two men who have left to fight return, unable to find each other in the dark; their movements should convey that they cannot see. (The original stage would not have been darkened.) Puck might lead Lysander right up to Demetrius's nose without one seeing the other. Their ears deceive them when they cannot see. Perhaps Puck makes a running noise by banging his hands on the stage causing Demetrius to think Lysander is fleeing (l. 405). The fairies might watch Puck deceive the men and join in: one could make the noise of a frog causing Lysander to move towards the sound only to find nothing there. The two men are led about the stage until, exhausted, they collapse. "In order to harry Lysander and Demetrius... [Brook's] Puck climb[ed] on six foot stilts and dart[ed] around the stage" (Thomson, p. 126).

PUCK   Follow me then
    To plainer° ground.   [*Exit* LYSANDER.]

Enter DEMETRIUS.

DEMETRIUS   Lysander, speak again!
    Thou runaway, thou coward, art thou fled?   405
    Speak! In some bush? Where dost thou hide thy head?

PUCK   Thou coward, art thou bragging to the stars,
    Telling the bushes that thou look'st for wars,
    And wilt not come? Come recreant! Come thou child!
    I'll whip thee with a rod. He is defiled   410
    That draws a sword on thee.

DEMETRIUS   Yea, art thou there?

PUCK   Follow my voice. We'll try no manhood here.
                                         [*Exeunt.*]

Enter LYSANDER.

LYSANDER   He goes before me and still dares me on:
    When I come where he calls, then he is gone;
    The villain is much lighter-heeled than I.   415
    I followed fast, but faster he did fly,
    That° fallen am I in dark uneven way,
    And here will rest me. [*Lies down.*] Come, thou gentle day,
    For if but once thou show me thy gray light,
    I'll find Demetrius and revenge this spite.   [*Sleeps.*]   420

[*Enter*] ROBIN [PUCK] *and* DEMETRIUS.

PUCK   Ho, ho, ho! Coward, why com'st thou not?

DEMETRIUS   Abide° me, if thou dar'st, for well I wot°
    Thou runn'st before me, shifting every place,
    And dar'st not stand° nor look me in the face.
    Where art thou now?

PUCK   Come hither. I am here.   425

DEMETRIUS   Nay then, thou mock'st me. Thou shalt buy this dear°
    If ever I thy face by daylight see.

more open

so that

418-30   At line 418 Puck puts Lysander to sleep and
then concentrates on Demetrius. Perhaps between
"Come hither" and "I am here" (l. 425) Puck moves,
speaking the second phrase from a new location,
maddening Demetrius with frustration. Puck sets up
where they sleep, drawing them to opposite sides of
the stage. To convey what they have been through,
by this point the lovers might be almost down to their
underwear, their clothes in tatters. Hall's Puck "blew
the fog out of his mouth; he put the men to sleep with
a snap of his fingers, the girls with a kiss" (Warren
1983, p. 51).

face, encounter with   know

make a stand, fight

pay dearly for this

Now go thy way. Faintness constraineth me
To measure out my length on this cold bed.
By day's approach look to be visited. [*Lies down and sleeps.*]   430

Enter HELENA.

HELENA O weary night, O long and tedious night,
Abate° thy hours! Shine comforts from the east,
That I may back to Athens by daylight,
From these that my poor company detest;
And sleep, that sometimes shuts up sorrow's eye,   435
Steal me awhile from mine own company.   [*Sleeps.*]

PUCK   Yet but three? Come one more:
                        Two of both kinds makes up four.
                        Here she comes, curst° and sad:
                        Cupid is a knavish lad,   440
                        Thus to make poor females mad.

Enter HERMIA.

HERMIA Never so weary, never so in woe;
Bedabbled with the dew and torn with briars,
I can no further crawl, no further go;
My legs can keep no pace with my desires.   445
Here will I rest me till the break of day.
Heavens shield Lysander, if they mean a fray!
                                   [*Lies down and sleeps.*]

PUCK   On the ground
                        Sleep sound.
                        I'll apply   450
                        To your eye,
                 Gentle lover, remedy.
                        [*Squeezing the juice on* LYSANDER's *eye.*]
                        When thou wak'st,
                        Thou tak'st   455
                        True delight
                        In the sight
                 Of thy former lady's eye:
                 And the country proverb known,
                 That every man should take his own,

cut short

431-63 When Helena wanders on Puck might react with delight that things are working out so well. Helena is lost; she does not see Demetrius or Lysander lying asleep, but perhaps she inadvertently heads straight for Lysander and is just about to lie down next to him when Puck intervenes. Fearful of making another mistake, he almost carries her over to Demetrius. Puck is tired himself and waits impatiently for Hermia to come in so his task will be complete. Hermia enters exhausted, collapses quickly and sleeps. The lovers seek to escape in sleep from the confusion they have gone through. Peaceful music might accompany the moment. Puck's simple verse and language is that of the nursery rhyme, and anticipates the final restoration of order. But after this vision of harmony, the action returns to confusion and madness.

ill-tempered, cross

In your waking shall be shown.   460
        Jack shall have Jill,
        Nought shall go ill;
The man shall have his mare again,° and all shall be well. [*Exit.*]

(another proverb)

ACT IV

Scene i.   [*Enter* Titania,] *Queen of Fairies, and* [Bottom *the*]
Clown, and Fairies [Peaseblossom, Cobweb, Moth, Mustardseed, *and
others*], *and* [Oberon,] *the King, behind them.*

[Lysander, Demetrius, Helena, *and* Hermia, *lying asleep.*]

TITANIA   Come sit thee down upon this flow'ry bed
　　　　While I thy amiable cheeks do coy,°
And stick musk-roses in thy sleek smooth head
　　　　And kiss thy fair large ears, my gentle joy.

BOTTOM   Where's Peaseblossom?   5

PEASEBLOSSOM   Ready.

BOTTOM   Scratch my head, Peaseblossom. Where's Monsieur
　　Cobweb?

COBWEB   Ready.

BOTTOM   Monsieur Cobweb, good monsieur, get you your
　　weapons in your hand and kill me a redhipped humblebee   10
　　on the top of a thistle; and, good monsieur, bring me the honey
　　bag. Do not fret yourself too much in the action, monsieur;
　　and, good monsieur, have a care the honey-bag break not; I
　　would be loath to have you overflown with a honey-bag,
　　signior. Where's Monsieur Mustardseed?   15

MUSTARDSEED   Ready.

BOTTOM   Give me your neaf,° Monsieur Mustardseed. Pray you,
　　leave your courtesy,° good monsieur.

MUSTARDSEED   What's your will?

BOTTOM   Nothing, good monsieur, but to help Cavalery°   20
　　Peaseblossom to scratch. I must to the barber's monsieur; for
　　methinks I am marvellous hairy about the face, and I am
　　such a tender ass, if my hair do but tickle me, I must scratch.

TITANIA   What, wilt thou hear some music, my sweet love?

BOTTOM   I have some reasonable good ear in music. Let's have   25
　　the tongs and the bones.°

caress

1-35 Oberon and Puck observe the action from the beginning of the scene and this colors to some degree the spectator's point of view. While there is still the fairy-tale element, this is a post-coital scene; it is not just cute and innocent. The emphasis is on the physical, as Titania's words indicate (ll. 2-4). Perhaps she cradles Bottom's head in her lap and strokes it while she listens to him adoringly. For Bottom this is a liberation of his senses and imagination; he behaves like a Turkish pasha. In his enjoyment and innocence he questions not.

fist

stop bowing, (?) replace your
   hat

Cavaliere (a gallant)

(crude percussion music:
   metal *tongs* were struck
   with a key; *bones*, or clap-
   pers, were held between fingers and so struck together)

TITANIA   Or say, sweet love, what thou desirest to eat.

BOTTOM   Truly, a peck° of provender. I could munch your good
    dry oats. Methinks I have a great desire to a bottle° of hay.
    Good hay, sweet hay, hath no fellow.   30

TITANIA   I have a venturous fairy that shall seek
    The squirrel's hoard, and fetch thee new nuts.

BOTTOM   I had rather have a handful or two of dried peas. But I
    pray you, let none of your people stir me: I have an exposition°
    of sleep come upon me.   35

TITANIA   Sleep thou, and I will wind thee in my arms.
    Fairies, be gone, and be all ways° away.   [*Exeunt* FAIRIES.]
    So doth the woodbine° the sweet honeysuckle
    Gently entwist; the female ivy so
    Enrings the barky fingers of the elm.   40
    O how I love thee! How I dote on thee!   [*They sleep.*]

Enter ROBIN GOODFELLOW [PUCK].

OBERON [*Advancing.*] Welcome, good Robin. See'st thou this
           sweet sight?
    Her dotage now I do begin to pity;
    For, meeting her of late behind the wood,
    Seeking sweet favours° for this hateful fool,   45
    I did upbraid her and fall out with her.
    For she his hairy temples then had rounded
    With coronet of fresh and fragrant flowers;
    And that same dew, which sometime on the buds
    Was wont to swell, like round and orient° pearls,   50
    Stood now within the pretty flouriets' eyes,
    Like tears that did their own disgrace bewail.
    When I had at my pleasure taunted her,
    And she in mild terms begged my patience,
    I then did ask of her her changeling child;   55
    Which straight she gave me, and her fairy sent
    To bear him to my bower in fairy land.
    And now I have the boy, I will undo
    This hateful imperfection of her eyes.
    And, gentle Puck, take this transformed scalp   60

(a measure = 2 gals. approx.)
bundle

(for "disposition")

in every direction
convolvulus

36-42 Titania's language and sexual images emphasize the idea of entwinement and suggest how she winds herself around Bottom as they fall asleep. When Oberon asks if Puck sees "this sweet sight" (l. 42), he speaks ironically, and perhaps sadly: he has, after all, conspired in his own cuckolding.

love-tokens (i.e., flowers)

from the East

53-59 Does Oberon have the boy with him as he speaks? There is no indication here or earlier when he and Titania fight over the boy that he is present, but directors often include him.

From off the head of this Athenian swain
That, he awaking when the other° do,
May all to Athens back again repair°
And think no more of this night's accidents
But as the fierce vexation° of a dream.   65
But first I will release the Fairy Queen.
    Be as thou wast wont to be;
    See as thou wast wont to see:
    Dian's bud° o'er Cupid's flower°
    Hath such force and blessèd power.   70
Now my Titania, wake you my sweet Queen.

TITANIA My Oberon, what visions have I seen!
Methought I was enamored of an ass.

OBERON There lies your love.

TITANIA   How came these things to pass?
O how mine eyes do loathe his visage now!   75

OBERON Silence° awhile. Robin, take off this head.
Titania, music call; and strike more dead
Than common sleep of all these five° the sense.

TITANIA Music, ho! Music such as charmeth sleep!

PUCK Now, when thou wak'st, with thine own fool's eyes peep. 80

OBERON Sound Music!   [*Music.*]
    Come my Queen, take hands with me
And rock the ground whereon these sleepers be.
    [*Dance.*]
Now thou and I are new in amity,
And will tomorrow midnight solemnly°
Dance in Duke Theseus' house triumphantly,°   85
And bless it to all fair prosperity.
There shall the pairs of faithful lovers be
Wedded, with Theseus, all in jollity.

PUCK   Fairy King, attend and mark:
    I do hear the morning lark.   90

OBERON   Then my queen, in silence sad°,
    Trip we after night's shade.

others
return

uneasiness, agitation

(?) Artemisia or wormwood
(Artemis is another name
for Diana)   Pansy (or
"love-in-idleness")

71-80   Oberon leans over Titania to administer the love-juice, and perhaps takes her into his arms, out of Bottom's. "My sweet queen" and "My Oberon" (71-72) indicate their mutual love and a return to their proper roles. Titania awakes confused, perhaps even horrified by what she sees (l. 75). She senses that something has happened to her but not what; it is a mystery she will carry with her for the rest of her life. Oberon's commands (ll. 76-78) show him taking control of the means to reconcile himself with his wife and sort out the other confusions.

(addressed to his attendants)

Bottom and the four lovers

81-98   Oberon and Titania now join hands and dance, probably in a roundel, symbolizing unity. "Rock[ing] the ground" (l. 82) suggests how the four lovers are lulled to sleep by the fairies' music and dance, in a ritualistic moment foreshadowing the end. The use of rhymed verse furthers the sense of "amity" (l. 83).

in celebration, ceremonially
in public triumph

sober

>   We the globe can compass soon,
>   Swifter than the wand'ring moon.

TITANIA   Come my lord, and in our flight   95
>   Tell me how it came this night
>   That I sleeping here was found
>   With these mortals on the ground.   [*Exeunt.*]

Enter THESEUS *and all his train;* [HIPPOLYTA, EGEUS.]
Wind horns.

THESEUS   Go one of you, find out the forester,
>   For now our observation° is performed;   100
>   And since we have the vaward° of the day,
>   My love shall hear the music of my hounds.
>   Uncouple° in the western valley; let them go.
>   Dispatch I say, and find the forester.   [*Exit an* ATTENDANT.*]
>   We will, fair Queen, up to the mountain's top,   105
>   And mark the musical confusion
>   Of hounds and echo in conjuction.

HIPPOLYTA   I was with Hercules° and Cadmus° once,
>   When in a wood of Crete they bayed° the bear
>   With hounds of Sparta: never did I hear   110
>   Such gallant chiding;° for, besides the groves,
>   The skies, the fountains°, every region near
>   Seemed all one mutual cry. I never heard
>   So musical a discord, such sweet thunder.

THESEUS   My hounds are bred out of the Spartan kind,   115
>   So flewed,° so sanded;° and their heads are hung
>   With ears that sweep away the morning dew;
>   Crook-kneed and dew-lapped like Thessalian bulls,
>   Slow in pursuit but matched in mouth like bells,
>   Each under each.° A cry° more tuneable°   120
>   Was never hallooed to nor cheered with horn
>   In Crete, in Sparta, nor in Thessaly.
>   Judge when you hear. But soft! What nymphs are these?

EGEUS   My lord, this is my daughter here asleep;
>   And this, Lysander; this Demetrius is;

125

observance (of the rite of May)
vanguard, earliest part

unleash

(said to have fought with
Theseus against the
Amazons)   founder of
Thebes (he lived long before
Theseus and Hippolyta)
brought to bay

barking
springs

having large, hanging chaps
sand-colored

i.e., the pitches of the hounds'
cry was varied, like a ring
of bells, some deeper than
others   pack of hounds
melodious

98-123 The sound of hunting horns signals the day, celebrates the coming of morning. For the first time since Act I, Theseus and Hippolyta return. If the same actors have played Oberon and Titania, some device is needed to cover the quick change required here. One way to do this is to have the horns blown and echoed, as the light changes to suggest the coming of day. Then some hunters—both male and female—might enter, adding to the new atmosphere. Brook solved the doubling problem "by having Oberon and Titania walk up to the stage doors, don cloaks and turn to walk downstage as Theseus and Hippolyta" (Thomson, p. 126). Hippolyta's responses to Theseus suggest that she has not given up her identity, but is willing to accommodate herself to a masculine world. The oxymorons (ll. 106, 114) convey the two-sidedness, and also the harmony that has been achieved.

The focus is on Hippolyta and Theseus but the lovers are still asleep on stage. The two might be above on the gallery, overlooking the lovers and hunters below. Hippolyta does not let Theseus control the discussion of hunting; for everything he says she has something to better him. Her references to Hercules and Cadmus (l. 108) are reminders that she is important in her own right—and a follower of Diana, the huntress.

This Helena, old Nedar's Helena.
I wonder of° their being here together.

THESEUS   No doubt they rose up early to observe
The rite of May and, hearing our intent,
Came here in grace of° our solemnity.   130
But speak, Egeus. Is not this the day
That Hermia should give answer of her choice?

EGEUS   It is, my lord.

THESEUS   Go bid the huntsmen wake them with their horns.
Shout within. They all start up. Wind horns.
Good morrow, friends. Saint Valentine° is past: 135
Begin these wood-birds but to couple now?

LYSANDER   Pardon my lord.

THESEUS   I pray you all stand up.
I know you two are rival enemies.
How comes this gentle concord in the world,
That hatred is so far from jealousy°   140
To sleep by hate° and fear no enmity?

LYSANDER   My lord, I shall reply amazedly,
Half sleep, half waking: but as yet, I swear,
I cannot truly say how I came here.
But (as I think) for truly would I speak—   145
And now I do bethink me so it is:
I came with Hermia hither. Our intent
Was to be gone from Athens, where we might
Without° the peril of the Athenian law…

EGEUS   Enough, enough my lord; you have enough.   150
I beg the law, the law upon his head.
They would have stol'n away; they would, Demetrius.
Thereby to have defeated° you and me,
You of your wife and me of my consent,
Of my consent that she should be your wife.   155

DEMETRIUS   My lord, fair Helen told me of their stealth,
Of this their purpose hither to this wood,
And I in fury hither followed them,
Fair Helena in fancy° following me.

at

to honor

(it was said that birds chose
their mates on Saint
Valentine's day, 14
February)

mistrust
object of hate

beyond

cheated

because of her love

128-49 Despite Theseus's earlier decree and the lovers' disobedience, all is forgiven in the new day. From here on Theseus is in control, but he is a different kind of ruler now; at lines 128-30 he speaks both ironically and indulgently. When the horns sound, the lovers awake with a start, surprised to find themselves lying where they are and with whom. They look up into the curious faces of the courtiers surrounding them.

Each of the four has a vague recollection of what has happened and the two men try to gather evidence, make sense of the experience rationally so it can be expressed. But Helena does not question, here or ever; she has Demetrius back, and that is all that matters. How can it be shown that Demetrius, unlike Lysander, is still under the influence of the love-juice? The lovers form two couples, making visual their new relationships. Knowing they have broken the law, they try to explain to Theseus, but, as a lover, he understands and thus forgives.

150-82 Egeus breaks in still demanding his rights; nothing has happened to him in the forest to change him. In the Brook production, when Theseus finished announcing that the lovers would be wed with him and Hippolyta (ll. 176-77), "Egeus stepped from where he had been standing between Theseus and Hippolyta and strode toward the exit.... He paused briefly, even expectantly, as he heard Theseus begin to speak again.... Once it was clear, however, that Theseus was simply announcing the cancellation of the hunting, Egeus continued to make his departure." He used a different exit from that used by Theseus, Hippolyta and the court to enter, "establish[ing] that he was withdrawing from Athenian society" (Maguire 1989, p. 105). Alternatively, Egeus might embrace his daughter, indicating his acceptance of Theseus's decision; or he might subside into sullen silence.

But, my good lord, I wot° not by what power   160
(But by some power it is) my love to Hermia,
Melted as the snow, seems to me now
As the remembrance of an idle gaud°
Which in my childhood I did dote upon;
And all the faith, the virtue° of my heart,   165
The object and the pleasure of mine eye,
Is only Helena. To her, my lord,
Was I betrothed ere I saw Hermia:
But, like a sickness,° did I loathe this food;
But, as in health, come to my natural taste,   170
Now I do wish it, love it, long for it,
And will for evermore be true to it.

THESEUS   Fair lovers, you are fortunately met.
    Of this discourse we more will hear anon.
    Egeus I will overbear your will,   175
    For in the temple by and by, with us
    These couples shall eternally be knit;
    And for the morning now is something worn,
    Our purposed hunting shall be set aside.
    Away with us to Athens! Three and three,   180
    We'll hold a feast in great solemnity.°
    Come Hippolyta.

            [*Exeunt* THESEUS, HIPPOLYTA, EGEUS, *and train.*]

DEMETRIUS   These things seem small and undistinguishable,
    Like far-off mountains turnèd into clouds.

HERMIA   Methinks I see these things with parted° eye,   185
    When everything seems double.

HELENA   So methinks:
    And I have found Demetrius like a jewel,
    Mine own and not mine own.°

DEMETRIUS   Are you sure
    That we are awake? It seems to me
    That yet we sleep, we dream. Do not you think   190
    The Duke was here and bid us follow him?

HERMIA   Yea, and my father.

HELENA   And Hippolyta.

know

foolish, trivial toy

essence

as in sickness

As in the first scene, Hippolyta is silent, but the actress can respond in such a way that suggests she had an influence on events: Hippolyta and the moon—Diana—are the moving spirits of the play. If Hippolyta and Theseus have been on the gallery, at "Fair lovers, you are fortunately met" (l. 173) they descend to the level of the others, becoming part of the group. The return to Athens is signalled, implying reintegration, the restoration of society through marriage. In contrast to the first scene, Hippolyta now exits with Theseus and the others.

festivity

divided (i.e., out of focus)

(she had *found* such a precious thing, that she cannot be sure it is hers)

183-96 The fragility of the lovers' experience is conveyed: the ease with which it can be distorted by memory and by trying to apply reason to it. Each has had a different experience and they try to put them together, grasping at things on which they agree. When they do, they know they are "awake" (l. 195). To help convey the sense of ongoing mystery, as the lovers leave the stage, hand in hand, they might let go of each others' hands and turn back, looking again at the place where they have had this strange experience, as if trying to make sense of it.

LYSANDER   And he did bid us follow to the temple.

DEMETRIUS   Why then, we are awake. Let's follow him,   195
    And by the way let us recount our dreams.   [*Exeunt.*]

BOTTOM [*Awaking.*] When my cue comes, call me and I will
    answer. My next is, "Most fair Pyramus." Heigh-ho! Peter
    Quince? Flute, the bellows mender? Snout, the tinker?
    Starveling? God's my life!° Stol'n hence and left me asleep!   200
    I have had a most rare vision. I have had a dream, past the
    wit of man to say what dream it was. Man is but an ass if
    he go about° to expound this dream. Methought I was —
    there is no man can tell what. Methought I was — and
    methought I had — but man is but a patched° fool if he   205
    will offer to say what methought I had. The eye of man hath
    not heard, the ear of man hath not seen, man's hand is not
    able to taste, his tongue to conceive, nor his heart to report,
    what my dream was.° I will get Peter Quince to write a ballad°
    of this dream. It shall be called "Bottom's Dream," because   210
    it hath no bottom;° and I will sing it in the latter end of a play,
    before the Duke. Peradventure to make it the more gracious,°
    I shall sing it at her death.°   [*Exit.*]

Scene ii   *Enter* QUINCE, FLUTE *and the rabble* [SNOUT, STARVELING].

QUINCE   Have you sent to Bottom's house? Is he come home yet?

STARVELING   He cannot be heard of. Out of doubt he is transported.°

FLUTE   If he come not, then the play is marred. It goes not forward,
    doth it?

QUINCE   It is not possible. You have not a man in all Athens able   5
    to discharge° Pyramus but he.

FLUTE   No, he hath simply the best wit° of any handicraft man in
    Athens.

QUINCE   Yea, and the best person° too; and he is a very paramour
    for a sweet voice.   10

FLUTE   You must say "paragon." A paramour is (God bless us!) a
    thing of nought.°

197-213 Bottom is between sleeping and waking, unaware that he has been enchanted; he wants to get on with the rehearsal. His speech develops slowly; it is not a continuous, flowing train of thought; he keeps pausing, trying to make sense of things, changing his approach. He might speak partly to the audience, partly to himself through the process of acceptance and denial. There is a shift after "asleep" (l. 200) as he remembers, realizes what might have happened, sensing that it was "a most rare vision." He then progresses to calling it a "dream" (l. 201), which grows out of the sense that it is something better left unexplored because it is too strange, mysterious. Perhaps he passes his hand across his head, touching his ears.

The urge to make sense of it prevails into "Methought" (l. 203), but again there is a turn, the negation of the possibility of understanding: "there is no man can tell what" (l. 204). This pattern of starting and stopping is repeated twice more. On the one hand, he would be crazy to think he had an ass's head; but on the other he has to acknowledge that something extraordinary has happened to him; he senses the mystery of it, as the biblical paraphrase suggests (l. 206-09).

After deciding to have Quince write a ballad, Bottom seems to have finished. At line 211 he might start to leave the stage, then turn to the audience with the idea of singing it at the end of the play for an epilogue. Again he seems to have finished, but there is a final flourish: the idea of singing it at Thisbe's death (l. 213) when the audience will be receptive to hearing about his vision. It will be the moment to give the audience release from the tragedy.

1-12 The four mechanicals are back home, believing that all their efforts and hopes have come to nothing. Quince, knowing his chance has gone, might sit center-stage, going over the script, with a big handkerchief, blowing his nose. When Starveling enters, having checked to see if Bottom has returned, Quince could eagerly rush up to him, asking his questions (l. 1). Starveling is probably not wholly distraught: Bottom's part is now available, he thinks. Flute asks what seems to Quince a silly question and he answers angrily. They despair: all seems lost.

Marginal glosses (left column):

(a mild oath: "God bless me")

attempt

(allusion to multi-colored motley of a fool's dress)

(garbled version of I Corinthians, ii. 9: "The eye hath not seen, and the ear not heard... the things which God hath prepared for them that love him") (news of strange events inspired many cheap broadsheet ballads)

has no reality/is endlessly profound

popular/holy

(presumably Thisbe's)

carried off (by the fairies)

perform/deliver

intelligence, judgment

appearance, presence

something wicked, shameful

Enter SNUG *the Joiner.*

SNUG   Masters, the Duke is coming from the temple, and there is
two or three lords and ladies more married. If our sport had
gone forward, we had all been made men.°   15

FLUTE   O sweet bully° Bottom! Thus hath he lost sixpence a day
during his life.° He could not have 'scaped sixpence a day. An°
the Duke had not given him sixpence a day for playing
Pyramus, I'll be hanged. He would have deserved it. Sixpence
a day in Pyramus, or nothing!   20

Enter BOTTOM.

BOTTOM   Where are these lads? Where are these hearts?

QUINCE   Bottom! O most courageous° day! O most happy hour!

BOTTOM   Masters, I am to discourse wonders: but ask me not what;
for if I tell you, I am not true Athenian. I will tell you everything, right as it fell out.   25

QUINCE   Let us hear, sweet Bottom.

BOTTOM   Not a word of me. All that I will tell you is that the Duke
hath dined. Get your apparel together, good strings° to your
beards, new ribbons to your pumps;° meet presently° at the
palace; every man look o'er his part; for the short and the   30
long is, our play is preferred.° In any case,° let Thisbe have
clean linen; and let not him that plays the lion pare his nails,
for they shall hang out for the lion's claws. And, most dear
actors, eat no onions nor garlic, for we are to utter sweet
breath; and I do not doubt but to hear them say it is a sweet   35
comedy. No more words. Away! Go away!   [*Exeunt.*]

set up for life

dear fine fellow

(a pension equal to a crafts-
man's wage)   if

13-20 The onrushing pace of the play, the need for haste, is again created by a series of entrances. Snug hurries in, excited, with the news that the marriages have already occurred. Flute's speech, perhaps given in tears, indicates how he admired Bottom. It is like an epitaph, an elegy. His praise focuses on the performance that might have been, the dream never to be realized—and an income.

brave, splendid

(to tie them on)
light shoes   immediately

recommended, chosen
    whatever happens

21-36 Just when everything seems lost, suddenly the mood lightens. When Bottom comes on shouting excitedly, they react in surprise and fear; the last time they saw him, he had an ass's head and they are afraid to believe what they see now. When they have just accepted the change in Bottom and his disappearance, he reappears as he was before. Their reactions are complex; it should not be just funny. They might look at one another, frozen, afraid to move at first, then rush up to Bottom, but not too near, remembering what has happened. Also, they have given up on their play and must readjust when Bottom reappears. Bottom's speech is a progression of ideas from saying he will not tell them to he will. The other four gather round eager to hear, looking at Bottom's head, trying to make sense of what they see. Bottom has a captive audience; perhaps he jumps up on the makeshift stage of boards and horses again. Now when Bottom takes over organizing the play, Quince is quite content; he encourages the others to listen to him. Bottom's "No more words" (l. 36) indicates they are still clamoring for information, fascinated by what has happened.

ACT V

Scene i.   *Enter* THESEUS, HIPPOLYTA, *and* PHILOSTRATE, [*Lords and attendants*].

HIPPOLYTA   'Tis strange, my Theseus, that these lovers
        speak of.

THESEUS   More strange than true. I never may believe
        These antique° fables, nor these fairy toys.°
        Lovers and madmen have such seething° brains,
        Such shaping fantasies, that apprehend°   5
        More than cool reason ever comprehends.°
        The lunatic, the lover and the poet
        Are of imagination all compact.°
        One sees more devils than vast hell can hold:
        That is the madman. The lover, all as frantic,   10
        Sees Helen's beauty in a brow of Egypt.°
        The poet's eye, in a fine frenzy° rolling,
        Doth glance from heaven to earth, from earth to heaven;
        And as imagination bodies forth°
        The forms of things unknown, the poet's pen   15
        Turns them to shapes and gives to airy nothing
        A local habitation and a name.
        Such tricks hath strong imagination
        That, if it would but apprehend some joy,
        It comprehends some bringer of that joy;   20
        Or in the night, imagining some fear,
        How easy is a bush supposed a bear!

HIPPOLYTA   But all the story of the night told over,°
        And all their minds transfigured so together,
        More witnesseth° than fancy's images,   25
        And grows to something of great constancy;
        But howsoever, strange and admirable.°

        Enter Lovers: LYSANDER, DEMETRIUS, HERMIA *and* HELENA.

THESEUS   Here come the lovers, full of joy and mirth.
        Joy, gentle friends! Joy and fresh days of love
        Accompany your hearts!

1-22   The action returns to the palace, but not the same masculine world of the first scene; it too has been transformed. Perhaps there are now flowers, gardens, trees added to the set, and some cushions to give softness. The mood is peaceful. Hippolyta invites Theseus to consider what happened in the woods, to consider another dimension of reality rather than dismissing it out-of-hand. Theseus does so, and he is smart; but he gives a very rational explanation. There is condescension in what he says but it is not an outright rejection.

ancient/grotesque ("antic")
  idle fancies, whims
agitated (like boiling liquids)
imagine
understands

composed

i.e., a gypsy's
delirious, extreme madness
  (ref. to *furor poeticus*)
gives bodily form to

recounted, accounted for

gives evidence of more

wonderful, marvelous

23-27   Hippolyta will not let it go at that. Theseus' speech is in the abstract; Hippolyta brings him back to the reality of what the lovers have experienced. Her response is part of the play's ongoing emphasis on the powers of the imagination. The masculine and feminine points of view are contrasted here. Hippolyta tells Theseus that there are things that are not explainable by reason but which should not be rejected. Her manner suggests that now they are married, Theseus must realize there is a feminine way to look at and interpret reality.

LYSANDER   More than to us   30
   Wait in your royal walks, your board, your bed!

THESEUS   Come now, what masques, what dances
        shall we have,
   To wear away this long age of three hours
   Between our after-supper° and bedtime?
   Where is our usual manager of mirth?   35
   What revels are in hand? Is there no play,
   To ease the anguish of a torturing hour?
   Call Philostrate.

PHILOSTRATE   Here, mighty Theseus.

THESEUS   Say, what abridgment° have you for this evening?
   What masque? What music? How shall we beguile   40
   The lazy time, if not with some delight?

PHILOSTRATE   There is a brief° how many sports are ripe:
   Make choice of which your Highness will see first.
                          [*Giving a paper.*]

THESEUS   "The battle with the Centaurs,° to be sung
   By an Athenian eunuch to the harp."   45
   We'll none of that. That have I told my love,
   In glory of my kinsman Hercules.
   "The riot of the tipsy Bacchanals,
   Tearing the Thracian singer° in their rage."
   That is an old device;° and it was played   50
   When I from Thebes came last a conqueror.
   "The thrice three Muses mourning for the death
   Of Learning, late deceased in beggary.°"
   That is some satire, keen and critical,°
   Not sorting with° a nuptial ceremony.   55
   "A tedious brief scene of young Pyramus
   And his love Thisbe; very tragical mirth."
   Merry and tragical? Tedious and brief?
   That is hot ice and wondrous strange snow.
   How shall we find the concord of this discord?   60

PHILOSTRATE   A play there is, my lord, some ten words long,
   Which is as brief as I have known a play;
   But by ten words, my lord, it is too long,
   Which makes it tedious. For in all the play

28-60 When the lovers enter, married, there is hand-shaking and kissing. Theseus is still impatient; he wants to do something to pass the time, until his wedding night (ll. 32-38). In considering possible entertainment he rejects those relating to his past (ll. 44-51), perhaps fearing they might remind Hippolyta of his exploits. The rest of the court hear him and pick up on his attitude. Theseus's amused description of the mechanicals' play echoes Quince's earlier oxymoronic description (I. ii. 9-10).

dessert or "banquet" of fruits and sweetmeats, following the main meal

pastime/shortened representation

summary

(Ovid's *Metamorphoses* tells how both Theseus and Hercules fought in this battle)

i.e., Orpheus (this tale is also in Ovid)

show, invention

(the poverty of scholars was proverbial)

critical, censorious

suitable for

61-80 Philostrate reveals himself to be a bit of a snob, and he assumes Theseus is too, but he is wrong. While Philostrate is right in his evaluation of the merit of the mechanicals' play, Theseus understands and appreciates their motives and effort.

There is not one word apt, one player fitted.   65
And tragical; my noble lord, it is,
For Pyramus therein doth kill himself.
Which when I saw rehearsed, I must confess,
Made mine eyes water; but more merry tears
The passion° of loud laughter never shed.   70

THESEUS   What are they that do play it?

PHILOSTRATE   Hard-handed men that work in Athens here,
Which never labored in their minds till now;
And now have toiled their unbreathed° memories
With this same play, against° your nuptial.   75

THESEUS   And we will hear it.

PHILOSTRATE   No, my noble lord;
It is not for you. I have heard it over,
And it is nothing, nothing in the world;
Unless you can find sport in their intents,
Extremely stretched and conned with cruel pain,   80
To do you service.

THESEUS   I will hear that play;
For never anything can be amiss,
When simpleness° and duty tender it.
Go bring them in and take your places, ladies.
                                        [*Exit* PHILOSTRATE.]

HIPPOLYTA   I love not to see wretchedness° o'ercharged,   85
And duty in his service perishing.

THESEUS   Why, gentle sweet, you shall see no such thing.

HIPPOLYTA   He says they can do nothing in this kind.

THESEUS   The kinder we, to give them thanks for nothing.
Our sport shall be to take° what they mistake: 90
And what poor duty cannot do, noble respect°
Takes it in might,° not merit.
Where I have come, great clerks° have purposèd
To greet me with premeditated welcomes;
Where I have seen them shiver and look pale,   95
Make periods in the midst of sentences,
Throttle their practised accent in their fears,

strong emotion

unpractised
in expectation of

sincerity, simplicity

persons in adversity

81-105 Perhaps as Philostrate is leaving the mechanicals enter and begin to set up props: a little curtain, a chair. In doing so they are observed by the onstage audience. Theseus sympathetically describes how the mechanicals feel, which helps lessen expectations before they begin to perform. It will be an unintentional burlesque and must be taken as such; to expect more will create disappointment. Theseus reveals his qualities as a ruler here.

accept/understand
magnanimity/proper attention
according to their abilities
scholars

And, in conclusion, dumbly have broke off,
Not paying me a welcome. Trust me, sweet,
Out of this silence yet I picked a welcome;   100
And in the modesty of fearful duty
I read as much as from the rattling tongue
Of saucy and audacious eloquence.
Love, therefore, and tongue-tied simplicity°
In least speak most to my capacity.°   105

[*Enter* PHILOSTRATE.]

PHILOSTRATE   So please your Grace, the Prologue is addressed.°

THESEUS   Let him approach.

Flourish of trumpets. Enter the PROLOGUE° [QUINCE].

PROLOGUE   If we offend, it is with our good will.
            That you should think, we come not to offend,
        But° with good will. To show our simple skill,   110
            That is the true beginning of our end.
        Consider then, we come but in despite.°
            We do not come, as minding to content you,
        Our true intent is. All for your delight,
            We are not here. That you should here repent you,   115
        The actors are at hand; and, by their show,°
            You shall know all that you are like to know.

THESEUS   This fellow doth not stand upon points.°

LYSANDER   He hath rid° his prologue like a rough colt; he knows
    not the stop.° A good moral, my lord: it is not enough to   120
    speak, but to speak true.

HIPPOLYTA   Indeed he hath played on this prologue like a child
    on a recorder— a sound, but not in government.°

THESEUS   His speech was like a tangled chain; nothing impaired,
    but all disordered. Who is next?   125

Enter PYRAMUS *and* THISBE *and* WALL *and*
MOONSHINE *and* LION.

sincerity/foolishness

understanding, comprehension

at the ready

(Quince's mispunctuation is corrected by omitting full-stops except after *end*, l. 111; an additional comma is needed after *come*, l. 109, semi-colon or colon at end of lines 110, 113, 114, and 115; *but in... come*, ll. 112-3 is in parenthesis)

on the contrary

ill-will

dumb-show, tableau

bother about punctuation, trifles

ridden/got rid of

sudden check in managing a horse/mark of punctuation

good order

108-17 The mechanicals have entered another world, one as magical and enchanting as the forest: a social world of manners and behavior of which they have no experience. They have never been in a palace and when they get there they are overcome, staring in awe at the food, the drink, the clothes. Perhaps the room is full of candles, creating a magical effect. The Pyramus and Thisbe play is a parody, but not for the mechanicals; for them it is a tragedy and they perform it as such.

While Quince gives the Prologue, the others are eager to get on, to start performing. Perhaps in their impatience they keep peeking out through the split in the middle of the curtain, pulling at it and pushing each other out of the way. They display the nervousness and excitment of inexperienced performers. Like high-school kids, the mechanicals take themselves and their play with deadly seriousness; their main objective is to do their best, least of all to be funny: they want to be brilliant, to impress their audience. Quince's prologue is complicated, and the more nervous he gets, the more he misreads it.

118-25 The onstage audience joke about the mechanicals' performance as a way of releasing the urge to burst into laughter. Everyone has had a couple of celebratory drinks, including the mechanicals, so it is a lively group; there is a general hubbub. If Egeus is present, the effect of events on him might be conveyed by his being drunk, a kind of escape. Brook's Theseus was grave and courteous to the mechanicals. The play was taken very seriously and there were few laughs; instead of heckling, the lovers participated, singing along with the mechanicals.

PROLOGUE   Gentles, perchance you wonder at this show;
                     But wonder on, till truth make all things plain.
          This man is Pyramus, if you would know;
                     This beauteous lady Thisbe is certain.°
          This man, with lime and roughcast, doth present   130
                     Wall, that vile Wall which did these lovers sunder;
          And through Wall's chink, poor souls, they are content
                     To whisper. At the which let no man wonder.
          This man, with lantern, dog, and bush of thorn,
                     Presenteth Moonshine; for, if you will know,   135
          By moonshine did these lovers think no scorn
                     To meet at Ninus' tomb, there, there to woo.
          This grisly beast, which Lion hight° by name,
                     The trusty Thisbe, coming first by night,
          Did scare away, or rather did affright;   140
                     And as she fled, her mantle she did fall,°
          Which Lion vile with bloody mouth did stain.
          Anon comes Pyramus, sweet youth and tall,°
                     And finds his trusty Thisbe's mantle slain:
          Whereat, with blade, with bloody blameful blade,   145
                     He bravely broached° his boiling bloody breast;
          And Thisbe, tarrying in mulberry° shade,
                     His dagger drew, and died. For all the rest,
          Let Lion, Moonshine, Wall, and lovers twain
                     At large° discourse while here they do remain.   150

THESEUS   I wonder if the lion be to speak.

DEMETRIUS   No wonder, my lord. One lion may, when many
          asses do.   *Exit* LION, THISBE, *and* MOONSHINE.

WALL   In this same interlude° it doth befall
          That I, one Snout by name, present° a wall;   155
          And such a wall, as I would have you think,
          That had in it a crannied hole or chink,
          Through which the lovers, Pyramus and Thisbe,
          Did whisper often very secretly.
          This loam, this roughcast, and this stone, doth show   160
          That I am that same wall: the truth is so.
          And this the cranny is, right and sinister,°
          Through which the fearful lovers are to whisper.

(archaic; accent on second syl-
lable: a comic rhyme)

126-50   As Quince summarizes the action the other
mechanicals enter in costume, and perhaps mime
the action Quince describes. Possibly Snug, seeing
the audience, has stagefright and stands there
unable to move.

is called (archaic)

drop

valiant

pierced (also used of tapping
liquor from cask)
mulberry (in Shakespeare's
source, the lovers agree to
tarry under a *mulberry* tree)
in full

play
represent

154-67   During the performance the mechanicals
could prompt each other, push one another on stage,
pull one another off. The naive honesty of the performers contrasts with the cynicism of the court. If
Wall overhears them being called "asses" (ll. 152-
53), he shows his hurt feelings. Perhaps carrying a
symbolic brick, Wall fulfils his role by stretching out
his hand, forming a circle with his thumb and forefinger to make the "chink" (l. 157). When Pyramus
enters, Theseus calls the courtiers to attention (l.
167).

left

THESEUS   Would you desire lime and hair to speak better?

DEMETRIUS   It is the wittiest° partition that ever I heard   165
   discourse, my lord.

THESEUS   Pyramus draws near the wall. Silence!

PYRAMUS   O grim-looked night! O night with hue so black!
   O night, which ever art when day is not!
     O night, O night! Alack, alack, alack,   170
       I fear my Thisbe's promise is forgot!
   And thou, O wall, O sweet, O lovely wall,
       That stand'st between her father's ground and mine,
   Thou wall, O wall, O sweet and lovely wall,
       Show me thy chink, to blink through with mine eyne!   175
           [WALL *holds up his fingers.*]
   Thanks, courteous wall. Jove shield thee well for this!
       But what see I? No Thisbe do I see.
   O wicked wall, through whom I see no bliss,
       Cursed be thy stones for thus deceiving me!

THESEUS   The wall, methinks, being sensible,° should curse   180
   again.°

PYRAMUS   No, in truth sir, he should not. "Deceiving me" is Thisbe's
   cue. She is to enter now, and I am to spy her through the wall.
   You shall see it will fall pat° as I told you. Yonder she comes.

Enter THISBE.

THISBE   O wall, full often hast thou heard my moans,   185
     For parting my fair Pyramus and me.
   My cherry lips have often kissed thy stones,
     Thy stones with lime and hair knit up in thee.

PYRAMUS   I see a voice: now will I to the chink,
     To spy an° I can hear my Thisbe's face.   190
   Thisbe!

THISBE   My love! thou art my love, I think.

PYRAMUS   Think what thou wilt, I am thy lover's grace;°
   And, like Limander,° am I trusty still.

THISBE   And I like Helen, till the Fates me kill.

most intelligent, rational

168-84 Earlier, when told what part he would play, Bottom said "...let the audience look to their eyes: I will move storms, I will condole in some measure" (I.ii. 19-20), and now he does his very best to live up to that description. Bottom pulls out all the stops, but while he is completely into his role as Pyramus, he is also still Bottom, breaking off Pyramus' heartfelt lament to respond to the Duke's comments, trying as always to control every aspect of the performance. There is little doubt that it will "fall pat" (l. 184) as Bottom says, since Pyramus' and Thisbe's actions are clearly directed by what they say. Perhaps, though, Wall misses his cue to show his "chink" (l. 175) and Pyramus must prod him, giving an amusing irony to the "thanks."

sentient
back, in return

exactly

185-200 When Thisbe mentions kissing Wall's stones, perhaps she actually does so, getting a mouth full of "lime and hair" (l. 187) and spitting it out. Pyramus and Thisbe speak to each other with Snout, as Wall, between them. Possibly Wall holds up his hand with his thumb and forefinger making a circle for them to talk through, and his arm gets tired and keeps slowly dropping so that Pyramus and Thisbe have to squat down or push Wall's arm up. Bottom and Flute are concentrating so hard on their performances that they barely notice. The combination of farce and earnestness is endearing.

if

gracious lover (blunder for "Leander")

PYRAMUS   Not Shafalus to Procrus° was so true.   195

THISBE   As Shafalus to Procrus, I to you.

PYRAMUS   O kiss me through the hole of this vile wall!

THISBE   I kiss the wall's hole, not your lips at all.

PYRAMUS   Wilt thou at Ninny's° tomb meet me straightway?

THISBE   'Tide° life, 'tide° death, I come without delay.   200
                              [*Exeunt* PYRAMUS *and* THISBE.]

WALL   Thus have I, Wall, my part dischargèd so;
              And, being done, thus wall away doth go.   [*Exit.*]

THESEUS   Now is the mural down between the two neighbors.

DEMETRIUS   No remedy, my lord, when walls are so wilful° to
        hear° without warning.   205

HIPPOLYTA   This is the silliest stuff that ever I heard.

THESEUS   The best in this kind° are but shadows;° and the worst
        are no worse, if imagination amend them.

HIPPOLYTA   It must be your imagination then, and not theirs.

THESEUS   If we imagine no worse of them than they of   210
        themselves, they may pass for excellent men. Here come
        two noble beasts in, a man and a lion.

                    Enter LION *and* MOONSHINE.

LION   You, ladies, you whose gentle hearts do fear
              The smallest monstrous mouse that creeps on floor,
        May now perchance both quake and tremble here,   215
              When lion rough in wildest rage doth roar.
        Then know that I as Snug the joiner am
        A lion fell,° nor else no lion's dam;
        For if I should as lion come in strife
        Into this place, twere pity on my life.   220

THESEUS   A very gentle beast, and of a good conscience.

DEMETRIUS   The very best at a beast, my lord, that e'er I saw.

LYSANDER   This lion is a very fox for his valor.

(for "Cephalus to Procris";
  Cephalus killed his faithful
  wife in error)

(see III.i.98-99)

come   come

eager, willing

(ref. to proverb, "walls have
  ears")

(i.e., actors)   illusions,
  reflected images, phantoms

203-12 The onstage audience is restless because
their imaginations and emotions are not engaged
and they are eager to continue the wedding celebration. Probably the lovers talk inaudibly amongst
themselves throughout the performance and need
only a little encouragement from Hippolyta and
Theseus to mock Quince's show. Theseus is polite
but patronizing and the others take their cue from
him.

fierce (pun on *fell* = "skin")

213-20 When Snug enters as Lion his fears dissi-
pate and he enjoys himself; he might pick a girl in the
court audience and play to her, looking for approval.
If so, Quince must drag him off stage when his part
is finished, but Snug keeps roaring and peering
through the curtain. Snug becomes a new man
through the experience of action—another kind of
transformation.

THESEUS   True; and a goose for his discretion.

DEMETRIUS   Not so, my lord; for his valor cannot carry° his   225
    discretion, and the fox carries the goose.

THESEUS   His discretion, I am sure, cannot carry his valor; for the
    goose carries not the fox. It is well: leave it to his discretion,
    and let us listen to the moon.

MOONSHINE   This lanthorn° doth the hornèd moon present—   230

DEMETRIUS   He should have worn the horns on his head.°

THESEUS   He is no crescent,° and his horns are invisible within the
    circumference.

MOONSHINE   This lanthorn doth the hornèd moon present;
    Myself the man i' th' moon do seem to be.   235

THESEUS   This is the greatest error of all the rest. The man should
    be put into the lanthorn; how is it else the man i' th' moon?

DEMETRIUS   He dares not come there for° the candle; for you see it
    is already in snuff.°

HIPPOLYTA   I am aweary of this moon. Would he would change! 240

THESEUS   It appears, by his small light of discretion, that he is in the
    wane; but yet in courtesy, in all reason, we must stay the time.

LYSANDER   Proceed, Moon.

MOONSHINE   All that I have to say is to tell you that the lanthorn is
    the moon; I, the man i' th' moon; this thorn bush, my thorn   245
    bush; and this dog, my dog.

DEMETRIUS   Why, all these should be in the lanthorn; for all
    these are in the moon. But silence: here comes Thisbe.

                                    Enter THISBE.

THISBE   This is old Ninny's tomb.° Where is my love?

LION   O!   [*The* LION *roars.* THISBE *runs off.*]   250

DEMETRIUS   Well roared, Lion.

THESEUS   Well run, Thisbe.

carry away

lantern (old form, indicating
  pun on *horn*)
(allusion to cuckold's *horns*)
i.e., growing fuller (Starveling's name indicates that he
  is very thin)

for fear of
in need of snuffing/angry

244-46 As Moonshine finally manages to say, he
comes on with lantern, thorn-bush and dog (sometimes real, sometimes stuffed). Perhaps he also
stands on something to put him above the rest, in the
sky, as it were.

249-57 In the Brook production "Snug, playing Lion
over enthusiastically, tumbled into the front row of the
stalls and clambered back on stage with profuse
apology to the audience" (Addenbrooke, p. 167); his
Lion really did alarm the ladies (Wardle). By contrast,
in Hall's 1962 version the timid lion's roar was a mur-
mur; all the onstage audience had to lean forward to
hear (Trewin, p. 514). In the 1959 production, "one of
their best moments occur[red] when Thisbe's cloak,
required by the Lion for the ritual mauling, remain[ed]
obstinately attached to her person" (Byrne, p. 554).

(indicating that the scene is
  now a different place; again
  Thisbe gets "Ninus" wrong)

HIPPOLYTA   Well shone, Moon. Truly, the moon shines with a
    good grace.   [*The* LION *shakes* THISBE'S *mantle, and exits.*]

THESEUS   Well moused, Lion.   255

DEMETRIUS   And then came Pyramus.

LYSANDER   And so the lion vanished.

Enter PYRAMUS.

PYRAMUS   Sweet Moon, I thank thee for thy sunny beams.
    I thank thee, Moon, for shining now so bright;
  For by thy gracious, golden, glittering gleams,   260
    I trust to take° of truest Thisbe sight.
          But stay: O spite!
          But mark, poor knight,
      What dreadful dole° is here!
          Eyes, do you see?   265
          How can it be?
    O dainty duck, O dear!
          Thy mantle good,
          What, stained with blood?
    Approach, ye Furies° fell!   270
          O Fates,° come, come!
          Cut thread and thrum;°
    Quail,° crush, conclude, and quell!°

THESEUS   This passion,° and the death of a dear friend, would go
    near to make a man look sad.   275

HIPPOLYTA   Beshrew my heart, but I pity the man.

PYRAMUS   O wherefore, Nature, didst thou lions frame?
    Since lion vile hath here deflow'red my dear,
  Which is—no, no!—which was the fairest dame
    That lived, that loved, that liked, that looked with cheer.°280
          Come, tears, confound;°
          Out, sword, and wound
        The pap of Pyramus:
          Ay, that left pap
          Where heart doth hop.   [*Stabs himself.*]   285
      Thus die I, thus, thus, thus.

obtain, catch

grief/destiny

258-92 Bottom might have begun his performance awkwardly, being intimidated by his surroundings, but he is completely confident now and shows his ability as an actor. The differences apparent earlier between Theseus and Hippolyta are again seen in their responses: regardless of the mechanicals' inept performances, Hippolyta's imagination is engaged. In the Brook production, when Theseus said this he "look[ed] across at Hippolyta, as if he [was] testing her." At her response, Theseus smiled, indicating that this was what he wanted to hear (Styan, p. 228).

avenging goddesses or spirits

three goddesses who spun, drew out, and cut the thread of life

good and bad together (the *thrum* is the tufted end of the *thread* where it is fastened to the loom; it is discarded when weaving is finished)

overpower   slay

deep feeling/passionate speech

face/cheerfulness

overpower, consume

                        Now am I dead,
                        Now am I fled;
                    My soul is in the sky.
                        Tongue, lose thy light;   290
                        Moon, take thy flight.

                                              [*Exit* MOONSHINE.]
                    Now die, die, die, die, die.   [*Dies.*]

DEMETRIUS   No die,° but an ace,° for him; for he is but one.

LYSANDER   Less than an ace, man; for he is dead, he is nothing.

THESEUS   With the help of a surgeon he might yet recover, and   295
   yet prove an ass.

HIPPOLYTA   How chance Moonshine is gone beforeThisbe comes
   back and finds her lover?

THESEUS   She will find him by starlight. Here she comes; and her
   passion ends the play.   300

                        Enter THISBE.

HIPPOLYTA   Methinks she should not use a long one for such a
   Pyramus. I hope she will be brief.

DEMETRIUS   A mote° will turn the balance, which Pyramus, which
   Thisbe, is the better; he for a man, God warr'nt° us; she for a
   woman, God bless us!   305

LYSANDER   She hath spied him already with those sweet eyes.

DEMETRIUS   And thus she means,° videlicet:°

THISBE   Asleep, my love?
                        What, dead, my dove?
                    O Pyramus, arise!   310
                        Speak, speak. Quite dumb?
                        Dead, dead? A tomb
                    Must cover thy sweet eyes.
                        These lily lips,
                        This cherry nose,   315
                    These yellow cowslip cheeks,
                        Are gone, are gone.
                        Lovers, make moan.
                    His eyes were green as leeks.

one of a pair of dice   single
    spot on a die (here pro-
    nounced to provide pun on
    ass, l. 296)

292-94   The repetition of "die" (l. 292) provides
Bottom with the chance to give five variations of the
action. In Hall's 1959 version, "Paul Hardwick's
beaming, self-satisfied Bottom finishe[d] off Pyramus
with a crescendo of five "'dies'" (Wardle). If Bottom
overhears the courtiers' comments he might look up
in hurt surprise. He has believed completely and
cannot understand why they are unmoved by
Pyramus' death.

minute particle
preserve

laments/lodges formal com-
    plaint/intends   namely
    (legal term)

308-31   Flute, as Thisbe, shows what he has learned
from Bottom. Perhaps he draws on the memory of his
sorrow at the supposed loss of Bottom when reacting
to Pyramus' death; he gives a convincing performance. Thisbe's death is a deeply felt experience at
the centre of an unfeeling audience; the mechanicals
not needed for the scene stand lost in the performance. Hall's Flute did not speak Thisbe's lines in
falsetto but in "a shamefaced baritone, and doubly
asserted his masculinity with a heavy pair of boots"
(Addenbrooke, p. 116).

       O Sisters Three,°   320
       Come, come to me,
   With hands as pale as milk;
       Lay them in gore,
       Since you have shore°
With shears his thread° of silk.   325
       Tongue, not a word.
       Come, trusty sword,
Come, blade, my breast imbrue!°   *[Stabs herself.]*
       And, farewell, friends.
       Thus Thisbe ends.   330
   Adieu, adieu, adieu.   *[Dies.]*

    [Enter LION, MOONSHINE, *and* WALL.]

THESEUS   Moonshine and Lion are left° to bury the dead.

DEMETRIUS   Ay, and Wall too.

BOTTOM   *[Starting up.]* No, I assure you; the wall is down that
    parted their fathers. Will it please you to see the   335
    epilogue, or to hear a Bergomask° dance between two of our
    company?

THESEUS   No epilogue, I pray you; for your play needs no excuse.
    Never excuse, for when the players are all dead, there need
    none to be blamed. Marry, if he that writ it had played   340
    Pyramus and hanged himself in Thisbe's garter, it would have
    been a fine tragedy: and so it is truly, and very notably dis-
    charged. But come, your Bergomask. Let your epilogue alone.
            [A dance.]
    The iron tongue° of midnight hath told° twelve:
    Lovers, to bed; 'tis almost fairy time.   345
    I fear we shall outsleep the coming morn
    As much as we this night have overwatched°:
    This palpable-gross° play hath well beguiled
    The heavy° gait of night. Sweet friends, to bed.
    A fortnight hold we this solemnity,°   350
    In nightly revels and new jollity.   *[Exeunt.]*

    Enter PUCK *[with a broom.]*

the Fates

(for "shorn"; misued for
   comic rhyme)
i.e., of life

stain with blood, pierce

i.e., remain alive

dance, probably clownish or
   rustic, in manner of
   Bergamo in N. Italy

334-43 When Bottom asks if they want to hear the epilogue, he might draw from his pocket a paper on which "Bottom's Dream" has been set down; when Theseus refuses the epilogue, Bottom's disappointment is apparent. At the end of the Pyramus and Thisbe play in Hall's 1962 production "Bottom stood triumphant and flushed, having given his greatest performance. In his ecstasy he dropped his ludicrous wooden sword; it lay between him and Theseus. There was a pause. The duke bent, picked it up, laid it in a graceful and chivalrous gesture across his left arm and, with a bow, presented it to Bottom. Their eyes meet for a moment. In that moment there was a 'gentle concord in the world" (Evans, p. 85).

i.e., of a bell   tolled, counted

stayed up late
obviously dull, coarse
slow
celebration

352-419 The fairy world concludes the play. The last moments can have the aura of a religious ceremony, with music, and people coming out with candles and a huge crystal bowl of dew, which is used very much like holy water, blessing the house and progeny to come. The foolishness of love and how the couples got together is not as important as the peace and balance which have been achieved: this world, which was in a state of chaos at the beginning, is restored. The restoration occurs because they have been transformed by the nightmare in the woods; and the purpose is to bring forth children: continuity.

PUCK   Now the hungry lion roars,
                    And the wolf behowls the moon;
              Whilst the heavy° plowman snores,
                    All with weary task fordone.°   355
              Now the wasted° brands do glow,
                    Whilst the screech owl, screeching loud,
              Puts the wretch that lies in woe
                    In remembrance of a shroud.
              Now it is the time of night   360
                    That the graves, all gaping wide,
              Every one lets forth his sprite,
                    In the churchway paths to glide;
              And we fairies, that do run
                    By the triple Hecate's° team°   365
              From the presence of the sun,
                    Following darkness like a dream,
              Now are frolic.° Not a mouse
                    Shall disturb this hallowed house:
              I am sent, with broom,° before,   370
                    To sweep the dust behind the door.

              Enter [OBERON,] *King and* [TITANIA,] *Queen of Fairies,*
                           with all their train.

OBERON   Through the house give glimmering light,
              By the dead and drowsy fire:
              Every elf and fairy sprite
              Hop as light as bird from briar;   375
              And this ditty, after me,
              Sing, and dance it trippingly,

TITANIA   First, rehearse your song by rote,°
              To each word a warbling note.
              Hand in hand, with fairy grace,   380
              Will we sing, and bless this place.
                           [*Song and Dance.*]
OBERON   Now, until the break of day,
              Through this house each fairy stray.
              To the best bride-bed° will we,
              Which by us shall blessèd be;   385

weary, drowsy
exhausted
used up, spent

(the goddess ruled as
   Proserpine in Hades, Diana
   on earth, Cynthia in heavens)   dragons drawing
   chariot
merry

(Puck's traditional task was to
   help with housecleaning)

372-403 The voyeurism of Oberon and Titania carries through the play even to the wedding night; they
are going to be there, watching. This creates a curious mixture of the erotic and the protective.

In the Hall production, when the fairies entered
to dance at the wedding, "they arrive[d] somersault-
ing and falling on the floor" (Brown 1960, p. 144).
"The various couples departed across the bridges
that led offstage from the gallery, pausing on them to

repeat from memory

bid each other goodnight. When they were gone, the
central trapdoor was flung up and Puck appeared.
The fairies suddenly materialised from everywhere,
and lit their tapers at the glowing 'wasted brands' of
the brazier left over from the play scene. Oberon lib-
erally distributed a shower of glitter dust which represented the consecrated field dew, and the fairies
processed up the stairs and through the house to
bless the sleepers with it. Oberon and Titania paused

(Theseus')

to kiss on the bridge that led to the 'best bride bed' of
Theseus and Hippolya" (Warren 1983, p. 54).

And the issue there create°
Ever shall be fortunate.
So shall all the couples three
Ever true in loving be;
And the blots of Nature's hand   390
Shall not in their issue stand.
Never mole, harelip, nor scar,
Nor mark prodigious,° such as are
Despisèd in nativity,
Shall upon their children be.   395
With this field-dew consecrate,°
Every fairy take his gait,°
And each several° chamber bless,
Through this palace, with sweet peace;
And the owner of it blest   400
Ever shall in safety rest.
Trip away; make no stay;
Meet me all by break of day.   [*Exeunt all but* PUCK.]

PUCK   If we shadows° have offended,
         Think but this, and all is mended: 405
         That you have but slumb'red here
         While these visions did appear.
         And this weak and idle theme,
         No more yielding but° a dream,
         Gentles, do not reprehend.   410
         If you pardon, we will mend;°
         And, as I am an honest Puck,
         If we have unearnèd luck
         Now to scape the serpent's tongue,°
         We will make amends ere long—   415
         Else the Puck a liar call.
         So good night unto you all.
         Give me your hands,° if we be friends,
         And Robin shall restore° amends.   [*Exit.*]

FINIS

created

ominous birth-mark

consecrated
way
separate

(see l. 207 above)

404-19 Puck speaks to the audience not as actor but as character; if we accept this, our imaginations are engaged until the last moment. In Brook's version, as Puck blessed the house, Titania and Oberon "strip[ped] off their wedding finery to face the audience" (H. Dawson). As Puck finished speaking, he and the other fairies "pelt[ed] up the theatre aisles shaking hands with the audience" (Wardle and H. Dawson).

giving, granting nothing more than
do better

i.e., hisses (from the audience)

(in applause)
make

Textual Notes

The Quarto edition of 1600, published by Thomas Fisher, must be the basis for any modern text of *A Midsummer Night's Dream*. A second Quarto edition published in 1619 was a reprint with no separate authority, although some corrections of obvious errors were made. Then in 1623, the play was published the third time in the one-volume collected edition of Shakespeare's *Comedies, Histories, and Tragedies*, known today as the First Folio. On this occasion Q2, the Second Quarto, was used as the printer's copy, but corrections and some additions were made, the latter chiefly of stage directions; these do have some authority since they quite frequently suggest that a copy of the play in use in the theatre had been consulted.

The First Quarto is a good text and seems to have been printed from a copy in the author's own handwriting. Some unusual spellings occur in other plays set from autograph manuscripts and in that part of the manuscript play of *Sir Thomas More* which has been judged, on other grounds as well, to have been written by Shakespeare. Signs that the copy was a rough or unfinished version are the irregularities among the entry directions (of the sort that a book-keeper in the theatre could not tolerate), variations among the speech headings, and some descriptive entries which could have derived only from an author writing for his own eye rather than the for actors: "*Enter the Clownes*"(III.i.1), "*Enter Theseus and all his traine*"(IV.i.105), and "*Enter-Quince, Flute, Thisby and the rabble*"(IV.ii.1) in which Flute and Thisbe are one and the same actor. Additionally there are some mislineations, especially in Act V, which are most easily explained as the result of some lines being written in the margin of the manuscript, as they were added during the author's revision.

The Folio text is not always able to improve on Q1. It reproduces numerous errors from Q2 and its corrections of readings from both Quartos are not always convincing. While correcting stage directions, the task was often muddled: for instance, the important addition of "*Enter Piramus with the Asse head*" in III.i was placed some nine lines too late; a line of text was printed as a stage direction; and four fairies were added when provision had already been made for them by name. In the dialogue some corrections are such that they must have derived in some way from the author and these have been retained in this and most other modern editions, as shown in detail in the collation which follows. Other corrections, however, could have been

mere guesses and these have usually been rejected; the more questionable
decisions are also recorded in the collation.

The Folio's division of the play into five Acts has been universally
accepted and is reproduced in this edition, together with the scene divisions
which have become traditional. The Folio's replacement of Philostrate by
Egeus in Act V probably represents a casting economy made by the King's
Men, but since this seems to have been governed only. by expediency, the
original allocation of lines has been preserved here. Its modification where-
by Theseus' lengthy reading of the "brief" detailing the various entertainments on offer (V.i.44-60) is shared with Lysander, so that the duke only
comments on each submission, may well represent another change by the
players; on the other hand it might have been Shakespeare's way of enliven-
ing the exposition. In this case this edition again stays with the Quarto, since
there can be little doubt that at one time this was Shakespeare's own arrange-
ment.

In the collation which follows readings accepted in place of the First
Quarto's are noted where they are of substantive importance. Changes in
punctuation or lineation are not usually recorded. Where an emendation
derives from the Folio this is marked by an "F" after the citation. Readings
derived from Q2 are not recorded as such. In all instances, the reading of this
edition is cited in italics; this is followed by the Quarto's reading, in roman
type.

Stage directions in the text amalgamate those in Q and F, using F's to
supplement Q's. Additions to both Q and F are marked by being printed
within square brackets in the text itself. The varying authority for stage
directions is not recorded in the collation except where the right choice is
open to question and of significance to the action or dialogue. Speech headings have been regularized without indicating this in the collation unless
some question arises.

I.i.   4 *wanes* wanes   10 *New-ben*t Now bent   24 *Stand forth,*
         Demetrius (inset in italic as S.D.)   26 *Stand forth, Lysander*
         (inset in italics as S.D.)   136 *low* loue   143 *momentary* F
         momentany   159 *remote* (Q) remou'd F   167 *to a* (Q) for a F
         187*Yours would* Your words   191 *I'd* ile   216 *sweet* sweld
         219 *stranger companies* strange companions

II.i.   61 *Fairies* Fairy   79 *Aegles* Eagles   91 *pelting* (Q) petty F
         109 *thin* chinne   158 *by the* F by   190 *slay... slayeth* stay...
         stayeth   201 *not, nor* F not, not

II.ii.   9, 13, 20, 24 (Speech headings not in Q)   30 *Be it* F Bet it
         43 *good* F god   47 *is* F it   141 *surfeit* F surfer

III.i.   26 *yourselves* F yourselfe   43 *SNOUT* ("Sn" in Q,F = ?
         SNUG)   47 *BOTTOM* F Cet   56 *and let* or let   75 *PUCK* F
         Quin   143 (Q as one speech, attributed to *Fairies*)   155-8 (Q
         as three lines: 1. *Fai.* Haile mortall, haile./ 2. *Fai.* Haile./ 3. *Fai.*
         Haile.)

III.ii. 19 *mimic* F Minnick   80 *I so* I   85 *sleep* slippe
         141 *congealed* F concealed   213 *first, like* first life   220
         passionate F (Q omits)   250 *prayers* praise   257 *no; he'll*
         no, sir, F   258 *he* you   264 *potion* (Q) poison F   299 *gen-*
         tlemen F gentleman   323 *she's* F she is   406 *Speak! In*
         Speake in   451 *To* (Q omits)

IV.i.   18 *courtesy* F curtsie   21 *Peaseblossom* Cobweb   69 *o'er*
         or   78 *sleep... five* sleepe:... these, fine   86 *prosperity* (Q)
         posterity   113 *Seemed* Seeme   121 *hallooed* hollows
         124 *this is* F this 168 *saw* see   196 *let us* F let's   203
         to expound F expound   205 *a patched* F patched a

IV.ii   2 *STARVELING* F Flut.

V.i.   34 *our* F or   44 *THESEUS* (F assigns lines in quotation marks
         to Lysander, 44-45, 48-49, 52-53, & 56-57)   188 *up in thee* F
         now againe   203 *mural down* Moon used; morall downe F
         260 *gleams* beames   303 *mote* moth   333 *BOTTOM* F Lyon
         352 *lion* Lyons   353 *behowls* beholds   400-1 (these two
         lines transposed in Q)

SHAKESCENES: SHAKESPEARE FOR TWO

The Shakespeare Scenebook

EDITED AND WITH AN INTRODUCTION BY JOHN RUSSELL BROWN

Thirty-five scenes are presented in newly edited texts, with notes which clarify meanings, topical references, puns, ambiguities, etc. Each scene has been chosen for its independent life requiring only the simplest of stage properties and the barest of spaces. A brief description of characters and situation prefaces each scene and is followed by a commentary which discusses its major acting challenges and opportunities.

paper ∎ ISBN 1-55783-049-5

✿APPLAUSE✿

SHAKESPEARE'S PLAYS IN PERFORMANCE by John Russell Brown

In this volume, John Russell Brown snatches Shakespeare from the clutches of dusty academics and thrusts him centerstage where he belongs—in performance.

Brown's thorough analysis of the theatrical experience of Shakespeare forcibly demonstrates how the text is brought to life: awakened, colored, emphasized, and extended by actors and audiences, designers and directors.

"A knowledge of what precisely can and should happen when a play is performed is, for me, the essential first step towards an understanding of Shakespeare."
—*from the Introduction by John Russell Brown*

paper•ISBN 1-55783-136-X•$14.95

APPLAUSE

RECYCLING SHAKESPEARE
by Charles Marowitz

Marowitz' irreverent approach to the bard is destined to outrage Shakespearean scholars across the globe. Marowitz rejects the notion that a "classic" is a sacrosanct entity fixed in time and bounded by its text. A living classic, according to Marowitz, should provoke lively response—even indignation!

In the same way that Shakespeare himself continued to meditate and transform his own ideas and the shape they took, Marowitz gives us license to continue that meditation in productions extrapolated from Shakespeare's work. Shakespeare becomes the greatest of all catalysts who stimulates a constant re-formulation of the fundamental questions of philosophy, history and meaning. Marowitz introduces us to Shakespeare as an active contemporary collaborator who strives with us to yield a vibrant contemporary theatre.

paper • ISBN: 1-55783-094-0

APPLAUSE

SOLILOQUY!

The Shakespeare Monologues
Edited by Michael Earley and Philippa Keil

At last, over 175 of Shakespeare's finest and most performable monologues taken from all 37 plays are here in two easy-to-use volumes (MEN and WOMEN). Selections travel the entire spectrum of the great dramatist's vision, from comedies and romances to tragedies, pathos and histories.

"Soliloquy is an excellent and comprehensive collection of Shakespeare's speeches. Not only are the monologues wide-ranging and varied, but they are superbly annotated. Each volume is prefaced by an informative and reassuring introduction, which explains the signals and signposts by which Shakespeare helps an actor on his journey through the text. It includes a very good explanation of blank verse, with excellent examples of irregularities which are specifically related to character and acting intentions. These two books are a must for any actor in search of a 'classical' audition piece."

ELIZABETH SMITH
Head of Voice & Speech
The Juilliard School

paper•MEN: ISBN 0-936839-78-3
WOMEN: ISBN 0936839-79-1

APPLAUSE